Professional Writing
in Context

Lessons from Teaching and
Consulting in Worlds of Work

Professional Writing in Context

Lessons from Teaching and Consulting in Worlds of Work

John Frederick Reynolds
City College of CUNY

Carolyn B. Matalene
University of South Carolina

Joyce Neff Magnotto
Old Dominion University

Donald C. Samson, Jr.
Radford University

Lynn Veach Sadler
Human Technology Interface, Ink

LEA LAWRENCE ERLBAUM ASSOCIATES, PUBLISHERS
1995 Hillsdale, New Jersey   Hove, UK

Lawrence Erlbaum Associates, Inc., Publishers
365 Broadway
Hillsdale, New Jersey 07642

Library of Congress Cataloging-in-Publication Data

Professional writing in context : lessons from teaching and consulting
    in worlds of work / by John Frederick Reynolds . . . [et al.].
        p.   cm.
    Includes bibliographical references and index.
    ISBN 0-8058-1726-3 (alk. paper). — ISBN 0-8058-1727-1 (pbk. :
alk. paper)
    1. English language—Rhetoric—Study and teaching. 2. English
language—Business English—Study and teaching. 3. English
language—Technical English—Study and teaching. 4. Technical
writing—Study and teaching. 5. Business writing—Study and
teaching. I. Reynolds, John Frederick, 1952–
PE1404.P665 1995   BK
808′.042′07—dc20 $22.50   94-23692
                                                              CIP

Books published by Lawrence Erlbaum Associates are printed on acid-free
paper, and their bindings are chosen for strength and durability.

Printed in the United States of America
10 9 8 7 6 5 4 3 2 1

31412148

Contents

v

Preface

This book about writing and its teaching—like most books about writing and its teaching, I suspect—has a story, and I don't want to belabor it, but I do want to tell it.

Carolyn Matalene and I had known and admired each other for several years, mostly for what we had written about writing, or written about teaching, or written about each other. And, as writers and teachers and friends often do, we decided to do something together. Something different. Something we thought needed to be done. Something about how our work-world experiences had transformed our thinking about writing and the teaching of writing. Something simple, straightforward, and reader-friendly. Substantive and informative, of course, but a little more "relaxed" and "accessible" than academic work tends to be, written in our "most natural" voices.

Then, as folks on such missions often do, we realized that there was probably more to be said than we could say by ourselves, so we got some of our friends to help us. Because my own work-world experience was primarily with for-profit corporations, and Carolyn's was primarily with state and local government agencies, and because we weren't completely sure (and wanted to find out) if writing issues remain pretty much the same from one work-world sector to another, we asked Joyce Magnotto to talk about her extensive work in federal bureaucracies, Don Samson to take on the high-tech firms about which he knows so much, and Lynn Veach Sadler (the only former writing teacher/college president/publisher/management consultant we know) to offer her uniquely broad perspective on institutions and workplaces in general.

The result was, of course, this book. We wrote our five respective parts independently; however, we conferred often and, practicing what we preach, sent multiple drafts of our individual pieces to each other for comments and criticisms and suggestions, which often led to dramatic revisions. That process, we thought, was a good way not to lose sight of our readers, whom we imagined throughout as being teacher–writer–editor–students like ourselves who constantly change roles while working together daily in workplaces and schools all across the country.

In circulating our drafts to each other, we discovered that there is much on which we agree completely, but some on which we just don't agree at all. We discovered that certain writing issues appear to change significantly from one workplace setting to another, but many others don't seem to change much. And we discovered that when the five of us write in our "most natural" voices, there are some things that end up sounding pretty good, and some things that end up sounding pretty annoying. No doubt you'll discover all of this yourself as you read our book. But whether you see the five of us as storytelling or editorializing, agreeing or disagreeing, telling you something new or telling you something you already know, amusing you or annoying you with the sounds of our voices, we hope that in the final analysis you find our book informative and our shared experiences useful.

The sharing of the information, after all, was the whole point. We thank senior editor Hollis Heimbouch and all the good people at Lawrence Erlbaum Associates for supporting our effort here and helping us accomplish our goal.

—Fred Reynolds

CHAPTER ONE

What Adult Work-World Writers Have Taught Me About Adult Work-World Writing

Fred Reynolds
City College of CUNY

About 22 years ago, as a university graduate teaching assistant, I taught my first writing course and, like most of my generation of writing teachers, was armed for the job with little more than a roll book, a coffee cup, a red Bic pen, a degree in literature, and the memory of what had been done unto me several years earlier. Thus, I showed my college freshmen lots of splendid excerpts from top-notch nonfiction prose, asked them to imitate those excerpts, and then passed judgment on their (mostly) five-paragraph themes after dutifully red-inking all AWK's, FRAG's, SP's, AGR's, CS's, RO's, FP's, and so forth. Later on, while working as a high school English teacher for two private college-preparatory schools, and having been evangelized by a workshop or two on the "New" Rhetoric, I "reformed" and, again, like most of my generation of teachers, abandoned five-paragraph romanticism and shifted my classroom focus (or so I thought) from critiquing compositions to promoting composing processes. My students brainstormed and clustered and freewrote and kept journals and combined sentences and endlessly revised, revised, revised, and I was really quite confident that I had finally learned how to do right by them.

I then left teaching and went to work for several years as a corporate communications officer for a computer services firm where, in a very writing-intensive job myself—a job in which I spent most of my days composing such things as letters, memos, reports, proposals, contracts, software documentation, operating manuals, press releases, speeches, sales brochures, and industry-specific magazine articles—I realized that most of what I had always taught my students about writing had precious little to do with the kinds of written work they would actually be called on to do as adults in the world of work. So I "reformed" again and, when I was given the opportunity to teach evening sections of writing courses for the local university, I leapt at it, and developed a course called "Writing for the World of Work"—at least until a new composition-program director told me I had to quit doing that because "it encroached on the turf of the business school," and "really wasn't quite what [she] had in mind for college-level writing courses, anyway."

Some years later, I left corporate America, returned to the world of schools and teaching, completed a doctorate in rhetoric and composition studies, and eventually became a full-time university professor teaching, among other things, courses in business, technical, scientific, and managerial writing. Along the way, I found that what I had learned about work-world writing during my own corporate years, and toyed with in that first "World of Work" course, was still being informed and refined by the limited but ongoing consulting work I was doing for businesses in the area. Most of this work involved little single-session workshops designed to improve the writing skills of doctors, salespeople, chamber of commerce groups, and so forth. Under consulting contracts, I also learned much from my own writing: such things as a lengthy recruitment brochure for NASA, several computer-user manuals for a high-tech firm, and, as part of an unusual research project prompted by my psychologist father-in-law, a book on writing problems in the mental health professions.[1]

But nothing—not my own prior corporate experience, my early forays into "World of Work" writing courses, my little "writing-skills workshops" for local businesses, my own professional writing work under consulting contracts, or my unusual mental-health research project—has so fundamentally transformed my thinking about the teaching of professional writing as what I have learned during the past 7 years or so from working very closely over extended periods of time with groups of adult work-world writers whose employers hired me "to help [them] do a better job." Here I want to focus on and share, in an informal and perhaps egregiously unscholarly way,[2] some of the conclusions I have drawn and lessons I have learned

---

[1]For one detailed book-length analysis of just how complicated writing and reading issues can be in a particular adult work-world discourse community, see *Writing and Reading Mental Health Records: Issues and Analysis.*

[2]I'm being more than a little facetious here, of course, but not gratuitously so; I think I need to make the point, right up front, that I know that what follows is no more and no less than a bunch of generalizations based on my own personal experience, and that some of my academic colleagues frown upon that "mode of inquiry." However, I genuinely believe that writing research need not be laden with disciplinary jargon, experimental mechanism, or theoretical "grounding" in order to be useful to scholars. Like many of my colleagues in rhetoric and composition studies, I find myself increasingly rejecting the "theory/practice" distinctions and methodological biases that have long troubled our field. See my "Motives, Metaphors, and Messages" for more of my thoughts on this subject.

from three particular groups of adult work-world writers who have most profoundly affected me and my university teaching. I offer this informal report, for whatever it might be worth, to the many teachers, students, writers, editors, managers, and consultants who share my interest in adult work-world writing issues.

SOME BACKGROUND INFORMATION

During the spring of 1988, I worked for several months on a wide range of writing problems and issues with 22 Boeing Military Airplane Company engineers, whose job was to provide ongoing engineering studies, impact analyses, and other technical advice to a Strategic Air Command located at Tinker Air Force Base in Oklahoma City. This delightful group ("I wonder where we learned to write in such an expansivist mode?") consisted of 17 men and 5 women (plus one spouse who started coming to our sessions because her husband told her it was fun), all of whom had earned under-graduate engineering degrees, and several of whom had earned one or more graduate degrees. Their work was quite writing-intensive, focusing on the constant production of letters, memos, narrative summaries of trips and meetings, and formal impact-analysis reports to the military. The members of the group were profoundly concerned with "being clearer," "being less wordy," "eliminating pronouns," "reducing the number of mistakes," and "pleasing the boss." "The boss" insisted on signing-off on all documents as if he had written them himself; I saw this as being a rhetorical oddity at the time but have since discovered it to be not so unusual.

In the spring of 1989 and then again in the fall of 1992, I worked extensively on writing issues with all 36 full-time employees of The Atlantic Group, a multimillion-dollar, privately held Virginia company that provided both tem-porary and permanent manpower for public utilities and nuclear services industries. This diverse and enthusiastic group (e.g., "We really ought to get together for encounter-therapy on our writing problems at least once a year!") included secretaries, marketing staff, personnel officers, proposal specialists, technical personnel, executives, even the president of the company, and was split pretty evenly by gender. Most of the group were college-educated, several of them in journalism or English, and about one third had earned M.B.A.s or other graduate degrees. Work at The Atlantic Group was, again, very writing-intensive, focusing on deadline-driven bids and proposals (both solicited and unsolicited), as well as the usual correspondence and narrative-summary reports on trips and meetings. The group members were anxious about "developing a coherent company form and style," as well as "writing faster with fewer mistakes."

From the fall of 1990 until the spring of 1992, I worked ongoingly, in three clusters of twelve, with most of the corporate officers in the Labor Relations Division of Norfolk Southern Corporation, a publicly-held Fortune 500 company headquartered in Norfolk, Virginia. This fascinating group of first-rate professionals included 35 men and one woman, all of whom spent much of their time writing intra- and extracompany correspondence, interpretive summaries of railway-labor-relations rules and agreements, reports on trips and meetings, abstracts of recent arbitration awards and judicial rulings, and "submissions," quasilegal briefs arguing the company's position in response to labor union appeals of disciplinary actions taken by the company against unionized employees. Educational backgrounds in the Labor Relations Division of Norfolk Southern were enormously diverse; some of the people I worked with had earned law degrees from Ivy League universities, while others had no formal education beyond high school (and a few had accomplished that by equivalency exam). Most had successfully completed, in some cases more than once, Norfolk Southern's excellent in-house "Effective Business Writing" course (which I, for obvious reasons, observed at length myself), but the general feeling among them was that it just didn't seem to help much with the specific kinds of writing done in the division.

In each of these three particular cases, I was originally contacted by people representing upper-level management, and asked how I might help them improve their employees' writing skills. I began my work in each case by asking the contact-person to collect and forward to me some representative samples, both "good" and "bad" in their opinion, of their employees' ongoing writing tasks, as well as individual writing samples (which sometimes, I should note, had to be procured on the sly by secretaries) from everyone with whom they wanted me to work. In each case, I spent a good deal of time assessing needs and designing materials before presenting a formal proposal to the contact-person. Once my proposal was accepted, I always began my work by meeting informally with the writers I would be coaching, mostly to introduce myself, deal head-on with people's anxieties and resistance, and gather information about writing attitudes, backgrounds, problems, and processes.

I learned four important things pretty quickly, have been enormously influenced by them, and believe they suggest some important directions for curricular reform in American secondary, post-secondary, and workplace writing education. (Please note also the discussion following the four points.)

1. All of these adult work-world writers told me that they write much more at work than they ever expected they would, and that the writing they do matters much more than they ever thought it would.

2. All of them felt, in retrospect, that they had had far too little serious writing instruction in school, both theoretically and practically, no matter how much schooling they had completed, and that what they *had* had didn't transfer very well to their world of work. What they remembered about writing from the world of school was that it focused on "the kind of writing

that none of [them] do anymore," and "petty rules" which were "never the same from one teacher to another." The rare few who had completed a business/technical/practical writing course in school said that it "didn't help much because the forms [they] learned aren't the way things are done here."

3. Almost all of the adults with whom I have worked said they drafted in longhand, very often incorporating boiler-plate chunks from previous documents, and then gave their drafts to secretaries who did a good deal of editing while preparing the final copy. (I strongly suspect that there are generational issues at work here, and that things are already well into the process of changing, but I did find this fascinating and believe our writing courses should discuss in some detail its implications for the writers, editors, and secretaries we are currently teaching.)

4. While writing problems obviously vary—sometimes dramatically— from one person to another, from one industry to another, and from one particular setting to another, I have come to the conclusion that there *are* certain constants; many useful generalizations can be made about adult work-world writing and, by focusing more of our attention on these basic issues, we can powerfully inform and transform our teaching of work-world and other writing courses in the years to come.

GENERAL TENDENCIES
OF ADULT WORK-WORLD WRITERS

Here, then, are what I have found to be the most basic issues:

Writers Tend to Underestimate the Complexity of the Task Facing Them, and Overestimate Their Ability to Manage It. Adult work-world writers tend to have complicated multiple readerships representing different needs, tastes, interests, and standards of excellence.[3] These complex writer/reader relationships create serious content, tone, and arrangement dilemmas. They also cause many of the writers' style and clarity problems. Adult work-world writers put too much faith in their ability to plan for all of this in their heads. Very often they struggle with trying to adjust to these complexities *while* they are in the process of writing, a process that is constantly disrupted and interrupted in the busy world of work.

Writers Tend to Focus Too Much on Microrhetorical or "Little-Picture" Issues Before the More Important Macrorhetorical or "Big-Picture" Issues Have Been Resolved. Adult work-world writers tend to focus entirely too much of their energies on correcting or editing

---

[3]I have found organizational communication (or writer–reader relationship) patterns to be far more varied and complex than the standard "spoke," "chain," and "pyramid" models that seem to dominate most of the professional writing textbooks I have used.

the original draft when what they very often need to do is completely refocus or restructure the original draft. I believe this tendency is largely the legacy of "current-traditional" school-writing instruction which, as most teachers of writing know, has been historically preoccupied by concerns about surface-level mechanical correctness rather than larger issues such as analyzing rhetorical situations and then adapting one's writing to specific audiences, purposes, and uses.

Writers Tend to Write in Indirect, Inductive, Narrative Arrangement Patterns. Because so much of the writing done by adult work-world writers involves summarizing and storytelling (or retelling), they tend to write just about everything that way, working up to and/or taking entirely too much time getting to the point.[4] This is very much at odds with everything we know about how readers tend to read, especially work-world readers for whom time is of the essence.

They Tend to Rely on What I Call "The One-Sentence Solution." Adult work-world writers tend to put far too many qualifiers, disclaimers, background information, context references and/or previous-document references, and complicated reasoning loops into single sentences. This inflates, smothers, and dehumanizes their writing style, impedes readability and, because it inevitably seems to lead to punctuation and agreement problems, is the single biggest cause of their "little-picture writing goofs."

Writers Tend to Ignore (or Relegate to Others) Document-Design Issues. Adult work-world writers tend to elevate the verbal over the visual, paying far too little attention to page-layout and design issues, which can dramatically affect reader motivation, attention, comprehension, and retention. Adult work-world writers have had almost no training in—and therefore don't seem to pay much attention to—what classical rhetoricians would call "delivery" (see, for example, Connors, and "Extra-Textual Features") or what technical communication scholars would call *cognitive readability* (see, for example, McAfee).

Writers Tend to Be Unable to Differentiate Between Rules, "House" Rules, and Tastes. Adult work-world writers tend to conflate and equate bonafide right/wrong issues—both macrorhetorical and microrhetorical— with institutional, disciplinary, supervisors', and previous teachers' preferences. (After years of being bombarded by various inconsistent editorial

---

[4]These natural "storytelling" tendencies, at least in my experience, are often exacerbated by "spillover effects" in workplace settings where "charter" or "dominant" corporate documents also happen to be narrative by their very nature.

rules and regulations, adult work-world writers tend to end up equating a "bonafide rule" such as "you have to use a singular verb with a singular subject" with a "house rule" such as "you always/never use a comma after the second item in a three-item series"; or a "taste," such as "you can't begin a sentence with 'however'.")

Writers Tend to Confuse Organizational-Dynamics Problems With Writing Problems.   Adult work-world writers tend to believe that the problems they have pleasing their colleagues, supervisors, and employers with their written work are the problems they have with writing. (And no wonder: supervisors and employers often hire consultants like me to help with "writing" problems that turn out to be organizational-dynamics problems.)

GENERAL STRATEGIES FOR ADULT WORK-WORLD WRITERS

The following strike me as being the most basic solutions:

Writers Need to Write More Reader-Oriented (Rather Than Writer-Oriented) Prose.   Adult work-world writers have good instincts, based on their own reading experiences, about how readers read; they should try to write that way. They should try to follow the "Golden Rule of Work-World Rhetoric": Do unto them as you wish they would do unto you.

Writers Need to Get a Better Fix on the Rhetorical Context of a Document Before They Start Writing It.   Adult work-world writers need to start their writing processes by addressing the "big-picture" issues. For example: Who are their readers (both now and later)? What are they trying to accomplish? What are the key issues they, as writers, need to clarify and stress? What are the traps they need to avoid? To what extent does the situation call for heightened attention to visual issues? (See Dragga for his incredibly useful "verbal/visual orientation heuristic" for dealing with attention to visual issues.)

Writers Need to Plan the Superstructures of Important Documents Before They Start Drafting Them.   Adult work-world writers need to use more planning guides, outlines, or what I call "chunking charts" as drafting guides—especially, I think, given the constant interruptions/disruptions of the writing process in the workplace. They need to remember that arrangement decisions have visual, logical, and rhetorical effects. When writers write in response to a particular piece of writing, they need to avoid allowing the arrangement of *it* to automatically control the arrangement of their response *to* it.

Writers Need to Place Key Ideas in Up-Front and Highlighted Positions. Adult work-world writers need to write more directly, deductively, and nonnarratively. They need to use more preview statements, and visual cues such as headings, boldings, bulletings, boxings, underlinings, etc. (as long as they use them wisely, sparingly, and consistently). They need to reduce the number of *visual-indexing cues*; that is, the number of imaginary vertical lines running down a given page. (It is for that reason alone that I urge work-world writers to type their correspondence in full-block format; this format reduces visual-indexing cues and ensures special visual attention for anything indented, offset, stack-listed, etc.)

Writers Need to Unpack, Deflate, Decompress, and Simplify Sentences. Adult work-world writers need to break the "one-sentence-solution" habit. As a revision strategy, they need to learn how to isolate their key idea, look at what is smothering or obscuring it, eliminate unnecessary or repetitive elements, and reconstruct what is left. Writers need to be shown how references, disclaimers, qualifiers, and so forth can be moved into parentheticals, footnotes, and separate sentences.

Writers Need to Be Vigilant About Both Common and Personal "Little-Picture" Error Patterns. Individual adult work-world writers need to learn how to identify and avoid their most chronic personal mechanical goofs and, as a group, they need to be on the lookout for semicolon goofs, comma-set goofs, and the confusion of similar words. In the process, writers need to come to a better understanding of the *differences* between rules, house rules, and tastes.

THE BIG PICTURE

The following are what I have found to be the most chronic adult work-world writing goofs at (a) the document level, (b) the sentence level, and (c) the word level. My implicit argument here, of course, is that professional writing instruction in both school and workplace settings ought to focus more on these major recurring problems than, as traditionally has been done, on business "forms" and a litany of "handbook rules":

1. CHRONIC DOCUMENT-LEVEL GOOFS:
   Wrong Tone
   Bloated Style

Poor Planning/Low Readability
Combinations of the First Three
2. CHRONIC SENTENCE-LEVEL GOOFS:
Tone and Bloat
One-Sentence Solutions
Semicolon/Comma-Set Patterns
3. CHRONIC WORD-LEVEL GOOFS:
Numbers
Odd Verb Situations
Similar Words

(Note: The documents and sentences that follow are all real and, in my opinion, representative examples of the basic goofs I am trying to illustrate. In all cases, however, actual names and so forth have been changed to protect the privacy of the writers.)

DOCUMENT-LEVEL GOOF #1: WRONG TONE

Letter 1, a letter from "Lou Ann Hitchcock" of the "Final Seasons Nursing Center," to my thinking profoundly illustrates the number-one document-level goof in work-world writing: *wrong tone.* Here is the context: Ms. Hitchcock is writing a letter in response to an earlier letter from me, in which I questioned an unexplained massive increase in supplies charges on an elderly relative's monthly nursing home bill. I am a long-time customer; the relative has been confined to a nursing home for more than 10 years, and is a private-pay customer to the tune of about $30,000 per year. To that extent, I consider myself worthy of a prompt, clear, and courteous response to my reasonable concern about monthly incontinency undergarment charges having suddenly tripled without explanation.

Although such things as sentence fragments, misspelled words, absent punctuation, cloudy language, and garbled syntax pervade the letter, the larger issue of concern is its *tone.* As an intelligent reader, I can decode the writer's answer to my question about the sudden jump in charges: Their business went on a new computer system and, as a result, the first subsequent bill included 45 days' worth of supplies charges rather than the normal 30. But wouldn't a simple statement to that effect (or even a quick phone call) have been preferable to this badly toned letter, which officiously informs me that "said recent statement . . . reflects average attend changes at 5.5 per 24 hour period which is very accurate of average," and that the business's new "computerized A/R system" has resulted in "improved cost recovery" for Final Seasons? Additionally, doesn't it say something about Lou Ann's

FINAL SEASONS NURSING CENTER

1200 WEST ROBERTSON   NORMAL, OKLAHOMA 73070   405-322-3200

November 15, 1994

Mr. Fred Reynolds
40 Rader St. #103
Norfolk, Virginia 23510

Dear Fred,

   Said recent statement in question reflected the first of being on the new computerized A/R system. Due to going on line with this changed cut-off dates. Whereas they had been from the 15th to the 15th.

   The result is this reflects 45 days ancillary charges as opposed to 30. A total of 250 attends therefore reflects average attend changes at 5.5 per 24 hour period which is very accurate of average.

   The dates of service therefore reflect the date the ancillary clerk key punches charged ancillaries rather than official date of useage. Also, changes you see are secondary to improved cost recovery.

   I trust this satisfactory answers your question. Calling my attention to this is appreciated as I did not know the run would contain these days charges and I'm sure other families will also have concerns.

                                          Sincerely,

                                          Lou Ann Hitchcock, RN

                                          Lou Ann Hitchcock, RN
                                          Administrator

LAH/pw

HEALTHNET
HEALTH CARE CORP.

FIG. 1.1. Letter 1, from "Lou Ann Hitchcock."

tone for her to have addressed me by my first name and yet signed her letter with special attention to her degree-status?

The result of Lou Ann's letter is that she has answered my question, but annoyed and offended me in the process. Her tone was wrong, given the situation that prompted her letter, and no amount of fine-tuning and error-editing can change that basic problem.

DOCUMENT-LEVEL GOOF #2: BLOATED STYLE

Letter 2, a "bread and butter" letter from "George Von Trapp" of "Invest, Inc." to the president of "Brokers Data Research" illustrates the *stylistic "bloat"* of much work-world writing. The context is that the president of the company has been talking with Von Trapp's consulting firm about writing a business plan and raising venture capital for an important expansion, and this letter is Von Trapp's courtesy follow-up stating that he looks forward to continuing to work with the reader.

Although the letter is attractive and error-free, it goes on and on about nothing. The only simple, straightforward sentence in the letter is the one near the end that says Von Trapp will "bring back the booklets" that "Mr. Thomas" wanted. The rest of the sentences in the letter make much rhetorical ado about nothing and, so, ironically, undermine the client's sense that Von Trapp is really the right person to help with clarifying goals and preparing a straightforward business-expansion plan for potential investors. A short (perhaps handwritten?) note would have been a much better strategy.

DOCUMENT-LEVEL GOOF #3:
POOR PLANNING/LOW READABILITY

Letters 3, 4, and 5 illustrate what I see as being yet another of the most basic faults of work-world writing at the document level: *poor planning* and, consequently, *low readability.* Letter 3, a disguised adaptation of an actual in-house Arbitration Award Summary at Norfolk Southern, was prompted by the writer's desire to notify a division executive, "Mr. E.T. Barnwell," about certain aspects of a recent Special Board of Adjustment ruling that the writer felt had very important implications for future labor-relations cases in the company.

Letter 3, its first incarnation, however, is poorly planned and exhausting to read. Its misspelled word ("superceded") and its absent apostrophe on "Organizations" are certainly not its essential problem. Rather, its monolith of undifferentiated single-spaced text offers no prereading cues whatsoever, and its few "signposters" (for example, "Two questions were are issue. The

INVEST, INC.

500 Classen Center, Suite 201
5400 Classen Boulevard
Oklahoma City, Oklahoma 73116
405-529-7600

July 8, 1992

Mr. Harvey M. Thomas
Brokers Data Research, Inc.
4100 N. Broadway
Oklahoma City, Oklahoma 73001

Dear Harvey:

Thank you very much for giving your time and attention for all our various discussions and focus groups over the last two or three months. **Several possible courses of action for assisting you in moving toward defining your objectives are apparent.**

I will appreciate meeting with you again soon for a short time so you can update me generally and specifically on the status of your proposed business expansion plans. General information about your current situation will be needed for my discussions with investors directed toward bringing into focus how your present objectives can be made relevant to their ongoing business planning and activities with the changes of direction that have occurred.

I'm looking forward to talking with you further . . . perhaps progress in your development of your business on ahead can be evolved out of additional discussion now, wherever you stand at this point in time. I plan to telephone you next week so that we can arrange a visit together at your office as soon as it's convenient for you. Also, at that time I'll bring back the booklets you wanted. I appreciate your consideration always and have particularly valued the opportunity for us to get to know each other and keep in contact about mutually beneficial opportunities.

Cordially,

Geo. Von Trapp

George Von Trapp

INVEST, INC.
Consulting and Management of Southwest Industry Investments
Corporate Development Strategic Planning Financial Analysis

FIG. 1.2. Letter 2, from "George Von Trapp."

SUBJECT: Summary of Arbitration Awards

Mr. E. T. Barnwell
Executive VP Operations

One award recently rendered by a May 5, 1988, Special Board of Adjustment,
Neutral Ben H. Edwin, ruled on a dispute between the Norfolk and Western Railway
(NKP) and The Brotherhood of Maintenance of Way Employees. A summary of the
award is as follows:

Two questions were at issue. The first addressed the question of whether the Carrier
may realign and/or consolidate Section Gang and/or Section Territories within a
Roadmasters District under the applicable Nickle Plate Agreements. The Board
managed to dispose of Question #1 by unduly narrowing the scope of the dispute to
only address the application of the 1954 and 1959 Mediation Agreements in relation
to realignment of section forces and their territories. The 1954 Agreement, which
required the Organizations concurrence to any such changes, was found to be
controlling in that there was no specific language in the 1959 Agreement which
granted the Carrier more latitude to make desired changes subject only to arbitration
regarding rates of pay when the changes increase the duties/responsibilities of
employees, to indicate that it superseded the 1954 Agreement. This view was given
preference due to the fact that the 1954 Agreement had "specific language dealing
with "abolish or rearrange sections" occurring "in the future" while the 1959
Agreement used more general language dealing with "material change in work
methods." Prior awards in similar disputes with decisions favorable to the Carrier
were discounted in that they did not address the issue of the applicability of the
Mediation Agreements involved herein and those awards were based on contractual
language that was not contained in the two agreements involved herein. Central to
the decision was that although sections have been reorganized in the past, the prior
record did not indicate that the issue of the Carrier's authority to make the changes
was acquiesced to by the organization. Past agreements between the Carrier and the
Organization in proposed realignments were found to have focused on wage rate
adjustments rather than the Carrier's overall authority to implement the change.

FIG. 1.3.   Letter 3. Arbitration award summary. First version.

first . . .") are buried in a deadening block of text that is insensitive to
readers' logical, visual, and rhetorical needs. The mere mention of this most
basic fault, however, prompted the writer to revise his letter into its much-
improved second incarnation, Letter 4. This version corrects minor errors
but, much more importantly, uses simple visual-highlighting strategies such
as bulleting, stack-listing, indentation, and underlining to give the reader an
up-front and ongoing sense of its plan, as well as a more readable report
on the issues at stake in the ruling.

SUBJECT: Summary of Arbitration Awards

Mr. E. T. Barnwell
Executive VP Operations

One Award recently rendered by a May 5, 1998 Special Board of Adjustment (Neutral Ben H. Edwin) ruled on a dispute between the Norfolk and Western Railway (NKP) and the Brotherhood of Maintenance of Way Employees in connection with a proposed rearrangement of section gangs. At issue were two questions which addressed whether under the applicable Nickle Plate Agreement:

- The Carrier may realign and/or consolidate section gangs and/or section territories, and

- There is any distinction between work in the Track Department which may be performed by employees assigned to a section gang versus that which may be performed by employees assigned to an extra gang.

In resolving the first question, the Board found that the 1954 Mediation Agreement, which required the Organization's concurrence with any such change, was still controlling. The Carrier's position that the 1959 Mediation Agreement, which granted the Carrier more latitude to make desired changes, is applicable, was discounted on the basis that:

- The 1954 Agreement specifically refers to "*abolish or rearrange sections*" while the 1959 Agreement is general in reference to "*Material Change in Work Methods.*"

- The right to make changes without the Organization's consent under the 1959 Mediation Agreement exists "subject to compliance with the collective agreement" and no special language in the 1959 Mediation Agreement shows that it supersedes the 1954 Mediation Agreement.

- The prior awards cited in a similar dispute on the Wabash which had a decision favorable to the Carrier was under a different agreement where the 1954 Mediation Agreement did not apply.

- The past reorganizations of sections on the NKP cited as being specifically resolved under the umbrella of the 1959 Mediation Agreement, which involved the parties coming to terms on rates of pay, contains no record of the Carrier's authority to make such changes being at issue; therefore, their showing is insufficient to overcome the *specific* language in the 1954 Mediation Agreement.

FIG. 1.4. Letter 4. Arbitration award summary. Revised version.

A & P Telephone
A Dell Atlantic Company

January 1, 1990

Dear Customer:

If you have a listing in the Southern States directory for telephone service that is outside A&P's service area, you may be affected by a change in how RONTEL listings are shown in the new Southern States directory which will be distributed this summer.

All RONTEL listings that begin with 238, 239, 244, 255, 421, 426, 427, 429, 430, 436, 468, 482, 547, 657, 721 will be shown as they appear in the RONTEL directory and will be interfiled with A&P listings in alphabetical order at no additional charge to you. If, in addition to the free alphabetical listing, you want your RONTEL number duplicated in an arrangement with your A&P number, you must call A&P and request the arrangement.

For instance, if under your main heading you want to have listed various locations and some of those locations have telephones with numbers that begin with 238, 239, 244, 255, 421, 426, 427, 429, 430, 436, 468, 482, 547, 657, 721 then you must tell A&P how you want those numbers to appear.

For each RONTEL listing we place in special arrangement with A&P numbers you will be charged $1.42 per month. In addition, there will be a one-time order processing fee of $37.20 to establish a separate billing account.

If you want a RONTEL listing duplicated in special arrangement with your A&P listing please call our listing center by April 7, 1990. The toll-free number is 800-431-5444.

Thank you.

A & P Telephone

FIG. 1.5. Letter 5. Example of a poorly planned, form-type letter.

Letter 5 illustrates a different kind of poor planning and low readability. Here the problem is not monolithic text, but faulty arrangement and unnecessary repetition of a litany of telephone-number exchanges to which the information applies. I remain unsure even to this day, but I believe the purpose of the letter is to notify certain phone-service customers that they must request (and, if so, pay for) dual-listing services in soon-to-be-revised business telephone directories. The form-letter tone of the letter (its "Dear Customer" salutation and anonymous corporate "signature") certainly adds to the reader's annoyance. The larger problem, however, is that the reader gets lost in the long list of potentially affected numbers (couldn't they be relegated to a footnote, a parenthetical, or a highlighted box at the top or bottom of the letter?). This long list complicates an already-garbled explanation of what's at stake. The writer instinctively knew that Paragraph 2, the first attempt at explanation, had failed; the "For instance" paragraph that follows tells us of the failure. The result of this poorly planned, low-readability letter is that its readers have no idea what they are being asked to decide, and few will likely call the toll-free number and request new (and income-generating) services from the company.

DOCUMENT-LEVEL GOOF #4: TOXIC COMBINATIONS OF THE THREE PREVIOUS GOOFS

Letter 6 illustrates well how these most basic document-level goofs in work-world writing—wrong tone, bloated style, poor planning, and low readability—are often combined in an unfortunate alliance. The letter is the cover letter or "letter-of-transmittal" accompanying (and, one would hope, clearly summarizing) the results of a "GMPK" audit commissioned by "Ronald Dennis" of "Pacific Pathways, Inc." A first-name salutation and first-name signature suggest that the principals in this communication are friends, and yet the tone of the text is clearly bloated "Accountant-ese." A deadening monolith of a single-spaced megaparagraph spins a garbled web of definitions, qualifiers, and disclaimers, which somehow are meant to provide a confidential report "solely for the use of managements (?) and others within the organization."

The actual receiver of this letter, the president of one of the companies with whose writers I had worked, sent it to me with a "post-it" note that read, "Huh?" I decoded it for him as best I could, and then filed it away for future use as a classic example of how a wrong tone and a bloated style can combine with poor planning and low readability to ruin an important piece of work-world writing.

Although bloated style to some extent requires attention to sentence- and word-level issues that I will discuss, my work-world consulting experience has convinced me that many of the tone problems, style problems, planning

GMPK

Certified Public Accountants
2200 Old Dominion Towers
Norfolk, Virginia 23555

July 29, 1994

CONFIDENTIAL

Mr. Ronald L. Dennis, President
Pacific Pathways, Incorporated
3200 Northwest Danson
Norfolk, Virginia 23510

Dear Ron:

We have audited the consolidated financial statements of Pacific Pathways, Incorporated and subsidiaries for the year ended June 27, 1994, and have issued our report thereon dated July 29, 1994. In planning and performing our audit of the financial statements of Pacific Pathways, Inc. and subsidiaries, we considered its internal control structure in order to determine our auditing procedures for the purpose of expressing our opinion on the financial statements and not to provide assurance on the internal control structure. A material weakness is a condition in which the design or operation of the specific internal control structure elements does not reduce to a relatively low level the risk that errors or irregularities in amounts that would be material in relation to the financial statements being audited may occur and not be detected within a timely period by employees in the normal course of performing their assigned functions. Our consideration of the internal control structure would not necessarily disclose all matters in the internal control structure that might be material weaknesses under standards established by the American Institute of Certified Public Accountants. However, we noted no matters involving the internal control structure and its operation that we consider to be material weaknesses as defined above.

This report is intended solely for the information and use of managements and others within the organization.

Very truly yours,
GMPK

Duncan

Duncan Candley, Partner

FIG. 1.6. Letter 6. Cover letter or "letter-of-transmittal."

problems, and readability problems that lead to document-level disasters can be significantly resolved if adult work-world writers will rely more on document planning guides such as the ones that follow. Each of these planning guides was designed by one of the actual adult work-world writers with whom I've worked during the past few years. My role in their development was limited to simply suggesting that the designers of the guides create customized forms they thought might be useful in planning their more important documents.

Guide 1 was developed by a writer who felt that he had particular trouble getting a prewriting "fix" on the right tone for his letters and reports. The writer's readers were multiple and varied in terms of position, readiness, attitude, and knowledge, so he designed a reader-profile planning guide to help him better adapt to specific readership situations.

Reader Profile

I. Position: boss/subordinate/peer/mixed

customer/supplier

public/private

2. Readiness: requested it

expecting it/not expecting it

3. Attitude: friendly/hostile/neutral/don't know

interested/uninterested/neutral/don't know

4. Knowledge: new business/old business

familiar with terms/unfamiliar with terms

5. Other: age

gender

etc.

FIG. 1.7. Guide 1: reader profile.

CORRESPONDENCE PLANNING GUIDE

File Reference: _____

Basic Purpose:

_____
_____
_____

Major Points I Want to Make:

_____
_____
_____
_____

Further Action Needed:

FIG. 1.8. Guide 2: correspondence planning.

Guide 2 was designed by a writer whose work focused primarily on correspondence. He felt that his major problem was that he would plan a letter in his head, begin drafting it, and then lose the sense of his plan because of constant disruptions of his writing process. After working with me, he designed a personal correspondence planning guide, which he could fill out prior to drafting and, more importantly, return to for guidance and refocusing whenever his drafting was interrupted.

Guide 3 was designed by a corporate writing team who collaborated on important proposals. Their purpose in designing this guide was to isolate and juxtapose customers' concerns and corresponding company answers so that they could "keep focused on [their] purpose whenever [they] got lost."

Guide 4 was a "chunking chart" that the Labor Relations officers of Norfolk Southern developed to visualize and guide the superstructural layout of their *submissions*, their elaborate briefs arguing the company's position in response to claims of unfair disciplinary actions against unionized employees. Because the writers of these documents tended so naturally to "get lost in the story" and "forget to argue the case," they developed this guide as their way of "seeing the big picture."

My point in presenting these writing guides is to illustrate that adult work-world writers are fully capable of developing their own strategies for solving their document-level writing problems, once those problems have been foregrounded for them. Similarly, their chronic sentence-level and word-level writing problems can be significantly resolved if basic, recurring "goofs" are explained to them in detail and not, as is often the case, buried

---

STRATEGIC PLAN FOR PROPOSAL

Customer's Concern #1:

Company's Proposal/Answer:

Customer's Concern #2:

Company's Proposal/Answer:

Customer's Concern #3:

Company's Proposal/Answer:

Customer's Concern #4:

Company's Proposal/Answer:

FIG. 1.9. Guide 3: proposal plan.

in a sweeping conventional treatment of grammar, punctuation, capitalization, usage, spelling, and style rules.

Here, then, are what I have found to be the most chronic sentence- and word-level goofs in writing done in the world of work:

SENTENCE-LEVEL GOOF #1: TONE AND BLOAT

Many adult work-world writers (like academics, perhaps) have somehow developed a perverse sense that professional writing has to be "qualified" and/or sound "intelligent" or "technical" or "factual rather than personal."

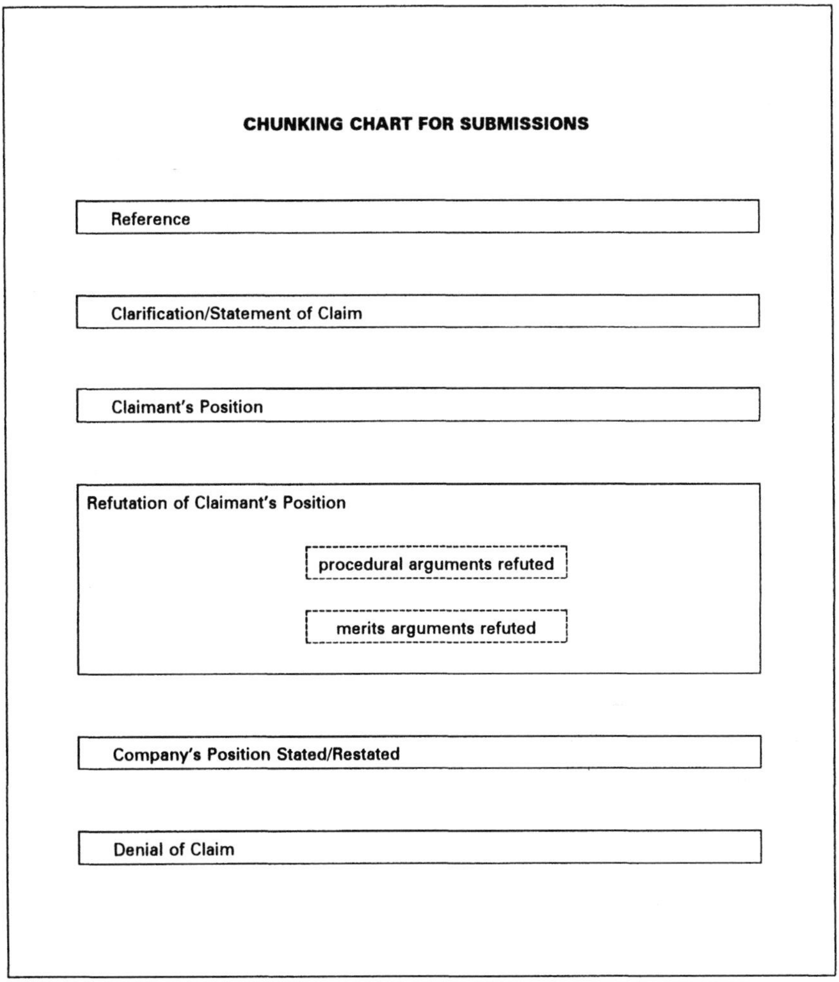

CHUNKING CHART FOR SUBMISSIONS

Reference

Clarification/Statement of Claim

Claimant's Position

Refutation of Claimant's Position

procedural arguments refuted

merits arguments refuted

Company's Position Stated/Restated

Denial of Claim

FIG. 1.10. Guide 4: "chunking chart."

Consequently such things as jargon, nominalization strings, rhetorical clouds and clutter, and heroic efforts to avoid the first person seem to pervade adult work-world prose. A simple sentence like "The 3211 can print reports" can "sound" so simple and, often, so dangerously unqualified, that the writer cannot resist the temptation to bloat it into "The 3211 is capable of printing reports" or "The 3211 provides the capability of printing reports" or "The 3211 is a device that provides the capability of performing the report printing function."

Consequently, I think that one of the most challenging tasks in working with adults in the world of work is getting them to rethink the whole tone/bloat issue by juxtaposing and analyzing excerpts such as the following, taken from a memo sent by a divisional executive to his department heads:

> "Employee performance criteria need evaluative review. Notations should be submitted for consideration prior to incorporation into manual updates ASAP."

In this example, the writer's tone is bloated and impersonal, and his heroic efforts to avoid pronouns (a corporate commonplace, in my experience, for reasons that largely baffle me) lead to a cold, unclear, and unmotivating request. With considerable coaxing, the writer ultimately produced the following excellent revision:

> "I'd like your input on revising the personnel manual. Why don't you take copy of the current manual and make some marginal notes where you think changes are needed? I'm especially interested in your ideas about the annual employee evaluation process. Because I have to meet a deadline myself, I need your suggestions by noon on Friday."

The key to this revision was what I call "putting the person back into the prose," something the adults with whom I have worked have been enormously reluctant to do. But, as is obvious in the revised version, the writer's request is clearer, as are his explicit suggestions about how to approach the task, and the reader is given a specific, human explanation for the "ASAP" factor.

SENTENCE-LEVEL GOOF #2:
THE ONE-SENTENCE SOLUTION

Most adult work-world writers with whom I've worked have an inordinate tendency to try to cram their point, why/how they have reached it, the extent to which they will disclaim it, and so forth into a single sentence. The result, especially when that tendency is combined with *tone, bloat,* and *jargon* problems, is sentences like these:

> "Due to the size and location of the LRU's in the antenna and receiver groups, practical maintainability must be continually addressed in equipment location, detail design, and development of test equipment, and so engineering studies must be accomplished to develop man-hour estimates to identify technical and program impacts in order that the system when installed performs as required and can be fully integrated into the aircraft mission support control environment."

"Interface with SSE and PSE technical personnel resulted in an exchange of information, including aircraft operating parameters when disparities occur, but interchangeability was checked and found to be interchangeable."

"Active service for rate progression will again commence at the expiration of an equivalent amount of time and training and rate progression will then be extended an equivalent amount of time and be applied to the rates of pay received."

"While the use of machinery in conjunction with line maintenance functions would remain as presently in effect under the agreement, all positions associated with the mechanized gang consists performing work described under herein (which would come under the authority of the Chief Engineer and include the rail train personnel) would be bulletined over the entire region and awarded on the basis of absolute seniority in rank (must be qualified on specific machine) irregardless of the employees relationship with an existing agreement."

Whatever else these sentences do wrong (there are a range of mechanical goofs imbedded in them), their most basic problem is that they are entirely too long. These writers have put too much into single sentences. I have tried a number of different things in approaching this problem, but I must confess that my most successful strategy for motivating adult writers to shorten their sentences has been to argue that it just "raises the reading-grade-level too high." Adults seem to accept the criticism that they're writing "too high" more readily than the criticism that they're writing "too long."

SENTENCE-LEVEL GOOF #3:
COMMA-SET/SEMICOLON PATTERNS

The most chronic and recurring mechanical sentence fault pervading the writing of the adults with whom I've worked is the failure to provide both commas of a comma set that marks off a parenthetical, or its variant, the failure to distinguish between the "stop-start" transition and the "parenthetical" transition. However, I've found it easy to make quick and enormous gains here: Once I have clearly explained what's going wrong, most of the adults with whom I've worked have stopped making the goof. The following are representative examples of variations on this fault:

"This claim is not supported by any provision contained in the agreement and is therefore, respectfully declined."

"This claim is not supported by any provision contained in the agreement, therefore it is declined."

"Claimant was required to file an injury report before leaving the property, nevertheless he did not file the report until ten days after the accident."

"Several provisions of the agreement have been changed, however, be sure to afford a five-day notice to the affected employees."

"Claimant admitted he improperly threw the switch and violated the ten-day notice rule, thus there is no basis for the claim."

"Personnel reductions however, may not be necessary if revenue projections prove to be accurate."

"Final decisions about downsizing need not be made until the first quarter of next year, however some personnel reductions will be required immediately if we are to maintain our profile in the market."

"We find ourselves largely as a result of third quarter losses, having to consider a wide range of downsizing options."

"If we are to maintain our position though, we must consider making some immediate changes even if projections are accurate."

In explaining the problem illustrated by these sentences, I have found it useful to hand out a list of transitional words and phrases, and then draw a diagram highlighting the difference between the "stop-start" transition and the "parenthetical" transition. "However" usually works best:

Two Sentences with a Stop-Start:

- ; however , - - - - - - - - - - - - - - - - - -.

vs.

One Sentence with an Interruption:

- , however , - - - - - - - - - - - - - - - - - -.

I found these to be the most common and chronic sentence-level faults in adult work-world writing. Similarly, I have found problems with numerical expressions, "odd verb situations," and easily confused similar words to be the most common word-level faults. Again, by targeting these major issues instead of covering everything in the typical business-writing handbook, I have almost always witnessed enormous gains.

WORD-LEVEL GOOF #1: NUMBERS

Adult work-world writers, in my experience, seem to have forgotten, or never gotten, basic guidelines for dealing with numerical expressions in prose and, unfortunately, adults tend to need these guidelines a lot for the kinds of work that they do. What they remember, sadly, is different teachers' preferences about some magic threshold at which a number has to become a word ("I learned it was anything over 10." "Well, I learned it was anything over 50."). The more important problems—internal consistency, clarity with decimals, numbers at sentence beginnings, mixed systems on dates and times, and cardinal/ordinal mixes—appear to have taken an educational back seat to anxieties and trivial disputes about the magic threshold. Here are some typical number-troubled sentences from the prose of those with whom I've worked:

"300 different parts must be inventoried at all times."

"2.975 man hours were expended at a PI ratio of .37."

(**Principle:** to avoid possible trouble later, sentences probably should begin with words, and decimals probably should be preceded by a zero.)

"The temperature fell 10 degrees in one and one-half hours."

"The development will be twenty-three miles of residential streets and 36 miles of access roads for municipal services."

(**Principle:** approaches ought to be consistent, at least within individual sentences.)

"Final data must be delivered by 10:30 on May 5th, 1988."

"Only 23 people showed up for our meeting at eight."

"Bids must be received no later than eight p.m."

"If you have questions, feel free to call me between nine and ten a.m. Monday through Friday."

(**Principle:** cardinals/ordinals and date/time systems shouldn't be mixed, and a.m./p.m. indicators are often critical.)

WORD-LEVEL GOOF #2: ODD VERB SITUATIONS

Except in cases where sentences had grown so long that the sheer distance between subject and predicate led to unintentional verb-agreement faults, most of the adults with whom I've worked have not really had chronic verb-agreement problems. What they *have* had problems with are what I refer to as "odd verb situations": compound, mixed-number subjects; neither/nor constructions; parentheticals that mask the true subject; clausal subjects; and those difficult "one of" versus "only one of" constructions. Here are representative examples of the kinds of sentences I have found to be troublesome for adult writers:

"The claimant, together with his fellow crew members, was/were guilty of not maintaining a proper lookout."

"Neither you nor your representative is/are right on this matter."

"It is you who is/are to blame for the accident."

"The facts, not your argument, give/gives credence to your position."

"What was involved here was/were instances of gross negligence."

"He is one of those employees who knows/know what the score is."

"You are the only one of the crew members who does/do that kind of work."

In dealing with such odd-verb situations, I give adult work-world writers this admittedly reductive advice: "If you've been sitting there very long, trying to figure out which verb is right, chances are that whatever you choose will sound wrong to someone, regardless; so I think you should reconstruct the sentence to avoid the odd-verb situation." I do try to explain the difference between the logic of the "one of" construction (the verb goes with the group) versus the logic of the "only one of" construction (the verb goes with the individual), but some students never quite comprehend any attempt to explain this logic, and so I move on.

WORD-LEVEL GOOF #3: THE CONFUSION
OF SIMILAR WORDS

Many of what have been described to me by supervisors as being *spelling* problems have, in fact, turned out to be *confusion of similar words* problems. The following memo (Fig. 1.11), which I have taken great pains to disguise (for reasons which will become obvious), was originally presented to me as an example of "serious spelling problems": This memo confuses similar words to the level of near-malapropism, and would be amusing if the issues being discussed weren't so serious. In working with adult work-world writers, I have typically spent some traditional "classroom" time discussing the differences between (or nonexistences of) the following:

anxious/eager
farther/further
fewer/less
principal/principle
enormity/enormousness
affect/effect
amount/number
cavalry/calvary
past/passed
imply/infer
advise/advice
council/counsel

November 3, 1993

TO: Department Heads

FROM: William F. Henson   *WFH*
                 Director of Personnel

RE: Miscellaneous Concerns

Now that we have past into our fourth quarter, I want to share with you some concerns that council has called to my attention.

They're principle concern is employee absenteeism. A large amount of staff have all ready used up most of their sick- and personal-leave days. Irregardless of whether or not these chronic absences are justifiable, the enormity of this problem is something I am anxious to discuss with you, since absenteeism could have a profound affect on our fourth-quarter performance.

A second concern on which I seek your advise is the apparently reoccuring (and perhaps related?) problems of positive drug-screen reports. Drug use, whether it be on or off site, is strictly prohibitive. In you're latest reports, however, you inferred that most employees believe drug use is acceptable so long as its not happening at work. We need to do something to insure that our colleagues know this is not correct.

Again, I am anxious to discuss these concerns with you at our meeting next week.

FIG. 1.11. Memo illustrating confusion of words.

    predominant/preponderant
    normal/normative
    prohibited/prohibitive
    regardless/irregardless
    it's/its
    your/you're
    their/there/they're
    occurred/recurred/reoccured/incurred
    assure/insure/ensure
    due to/since/because
    all ready/already

I have found that discussing these similar words in detail resolves many "spelling" problems. (Keep in mind that "spelling check" functions of word-processing systems will never detect most of these goofs.) And in studying participant evaluation forms, I have also found my discussion of similar-word confusions to be one of the most popular elements of my corporate writing workshops.

SOME FINAL COMMENTS

Although my focus throughout this chapter has been almost exclusively on the common, chronic, shared problems and subsequent generalizations I can make about adult work-world writing based on my years of working with adult work-world writers, I do want to discuss some other issues, many of them organizational-dynamics problems that often manifest themselves as "writing" problems in worlds of work. Here I will offer some examples of some of the kinds of issues I have raised in my final reports to the supervisors who have hired me to help their employees improve their writing skills. My sense is that these, too, may be useful to those interested in working now or in the future with adult work-world writers.

Other Miscellaneous Work-World Writing Problems

1. I found some real oddities-of-context for some of the writers with whom I worked, especially the labor-relations officers. In addition to the fairly predictable constraints these adults had to work with, they also had to cope with the odd fact that they often had no real rhetorical goal. Often, for example, they knew from the start that they had no realistic chance of persuading their reader(s), but they had to pretend they did anyway, and they found the pretense difficult. Also, they often *wanted* to be unclear; their goal, they often thought, was to "confuse the enemy." Oddities-of-context such as these cut people off, I think, from their rhetorical instincts; their gut-level intuitions fail them in these cases. Adults might benefit from more training in what some writing teachers call "rhetorical play-like" ("pretend you are X imaginary person writing to Y imaginary person about Z imaginary issue").

2. I often found widespread "we can't do that" anxieties and worries that I thought needed confronting by someone other than me. In all of the settings in which I coached adult writers, certain corporate and divisional writing conventions had obviously emerged over time (for example, in the labor relations setting, "merits arguments must come before procedural arguments" and "responses must be arranged according to the order of a claimant's arguments"), and many of these could be traced back to individual leaders' tastes, rather than to bonafide rules or well thought-out strategies. I felt that everyone involved—the writers, the supervisors, the executives, and the secretaries—would benefit from further discussions of what I like to call "rules versus tastes" issues.

3. I found that many of the people I worked with were very defensive about their writing, and for two especially powerful and understandable reasons. First, many of the writers were affected by a troublesome corporate class-consciousness based on education. Some of the people I worked with were convinced that they didn't write well because they didn't have a college education, whereas others believed they wrote well because they had earned a graduate or professional degree. The relationship between educational level and writing ability is, of course, not an absolute one, perhaps evidenced best by the number of academics with doctorates who have trouble writing clear and compelling prose. The myth, however, prevails, endures, and causes trouble. I almost always felt that much more could be done to remind people that all of us can learn to write more effectively, regardless of our level of formal education. Second, I often ran into troublesome beliefs that only bad writing gets attention. There was a perception at Norfolk Southern, for example, that, if an officer won a case, the praise would never focus on his good writing skills, but, if he lost a case, the blame would always focus on his poor writing skills. Perceptions such as these need confronting, I think, because they undermine written work in corporate settings. They do a great disservice to people at both ends of the writing-talent spectrum; less accomplished writers will continue to feel that they lack basic skills others have, and more accomplished writers will continue to feel that their talent is in no way special.

4. I found that several of the more talented writers I worked with genu-inely did not understand why some of their colleagues didn't write very well. I believe that management-level and implicitly supervisory people need to be better informed about the sources of, causes of, and possible solutions to the chronic and recurring error patterns in their colleagues' writing. I am convinced that exciting new leadership opportunities can emerge from this process. At the end of one of my workshop cyles, for example, one person told me privately that he wished I had spent more time teaching him strate-gies for helping others improve. I felt that the company involved in this case could benefit from having me, or someone else, help them capitalize on opportunities to move their own people into peer-coaching roles.[5]

5. I almost always felt that the people I worked with would benefit from having a heightened awareness and more control of document arrangement and presentation (visual emphasis) issues while they were in the process of writing. In several corporate settings, then, I felt that converting to PC-based word-processing systems would be a useful move.[6] From my perspective,

---

[5]I'm pleased to report that one of the companies I worked with has just recently done precisely that.

[6]I'm pleased to report that one of the companies I worked with has recently done that, too—and with great success, I am told.

such conversions are inevitable, anyway, because the next generation of
adult work-world writers are likely be more and more computer-dependent,
even disabled, without personal computers at which to write.

6. I found that many of the people I worked with had really special
rhetorical gifts. Two had the best senses of written logic and argument layout
I have ever seen. Another was very gifted at the subtleties of persuasive
style. Many were near-perfect spellers and punctuators. I felt that the companies I worked with should harness the potential power of putting their
people into writing teams based on well-matched rhetorical strengths and
weaknesses.[7] Many of the people I worked with were already very good
writers, but many others were especially good learners, and I often felt that
big gains could be made by capitalizing on their motivation while continuing
to work with them.

THE LAST WORD(S): MY WISH-LIST

By now, it should be clear that throughout this discussion I have been
arguing, at least implicitly, for certain reforms in American writing education.
I will conclude, then, by being explicit: My work-world teaching/consulting
experience has led me to the inevitable conclusion that we need to fundamentally re-think how we teach professional (and other) writing courses in
the world of schools. The personal wish-list that follows would be, I think,
a good place for us to start:

1. I wish that people would write more in school, and that at least some
   of that writing would be work-world oriented.
2. I wish that school-writing instruction would focus more on basic issues,
   and that it would emphasize macrorhetorical (big-picture) rather than
   microrhetorical (little-picture) problems and strategies.
3. I wish that those who taught (and those who took) professional writing
   courses in school would be much better prepared for the task facing
   them.[8]
4. I wish that we would enter into more work-world/school-world partnerships. Where writing is concerned, schools can help workplaces,

---

[7]See notes 5 and 6. Ditto.

[8]Despite all our progress in composition studies since I was a graduate teaching assistant
22 years ago, and despite the rising number of college-level programs and courses and textbooks
in business/technical/professional writing, the land of "practical" writing studies—like the land
of first-year college composition, perhaps—remains a troublesome hodge-podge of competing
instructional priorities and agendas and, in far too many cases, a land heavily populated by
underprepared students *and teachers*. See Matalene's *Worlds of Writing* and my own "Classical
Rhetoric and the Teaching of Technical Writing" for their critiques of current professional writing
courses and textbooks.

and workplaces can help schools, but we have only barely begun to explore the possibilities. The longstanding "school-world versus real-world" distinction that impedes us seems silly, outdated, inefficient, and unproductive to me. After 22 years of experience, I find myself wishing more and more that *our* world of work—through internships, co-ops, staff exchanges, various reciprocities, and "trades" and such—would collaborate more on teaching, learning, and researching projects with the *larger* world of work that we inevitably, sooner or later, serve.

ACKNOWLEDGMENTS

Many to whom I am much indebted must go unnamed here; however, I can and do thank Frank Ward, Curt Steele, Tom Mullenix, Mel Miller, Alan Sonner, and Elaine Dawson.

WORKS CITED

Connors, Robert J. "*Actio*: A Rhetoric of Written Delivery (Iteration Two)." *Rhetorical Memory and Delivery: Classical Concepts for Contemporary Composition and Communication*. Ed. John Frederick Reynolds. Hillsdale, NJ: Lawrence Erlbaum Associates, 1993. 65–77.

Dragga, Sam, and Gwendolyn Gong. *Editing: The Design of Rhetoric*. Amityville, NY: Baywood Publishing, 1989.

Matalene, Carolyn B. *Worlds of Writing: Teaching and Learning in Discourse Communities of Work*. New York: Random House, 1989.

McAfee, Christine O'Leary. "Cognitive Readability and Desktop Publishing." *Computer-Assisted Composition Journal* 6 (1992): 33–36.

Reynolds, John Frederick. "Classical Rhetoric and Computer-Assisted Composition: Extra-Textual Features as 'Delivery.' " *Computer-Assisted Composition Journal* 3 (1989): 101–107.

———. "Classical Rhetoric and the Teaching of Technical Writing." *Technical Communication Quarterly* 1 (1992): 63–76.

———. "Motives, Metaphors, and Messages in Critical Receptions of Experimental Research: A Comment with Postscript." *Journal of Advanced Composition* 10 (1990): 110–116.

———, David C. Mair, and Pamela C. Fischer. *Writing and Reading Mental Health Records: Issues and Analysis*. Newbury Park, CA: Sage Publications, 1992.

CHAPTER TWO

Of the People, by the People, for the People: Texts in Public Contexts

Carolyn Matalene
University of South Carolina

THE CONTEXT

The University of South Carolina, founded in 1801, is not only one of the oldest public universities in the country, it is also one of the few located literally next door to the state legislature that funds it. The university and the State House sit side by side in downtown Columbia, their classroom and office buildings almost intermingled. This closeness makes for a sometimes symbiotic relationship; undergraduates leave their classes to dash to the State House for duties as pages, and some eventually serve as researchers and interns for Senate and House committees. State employees can complete graduate degrees after their working hours in the university's Masters in Public Administration program. And the state's Executive Leadership Institute holds sessions on the university campus, using faculty members as instructors. Faculty members are asked to serve on state boards and commissions, and prominent political leaders occasionally teach a course when they leave office. Thus, although legislators and faculty members traditionally think of each other as coming from different planets, state government and the university are more than just neighbors. Some observers have noted, however, that the government buildings face outward, displaying their columns and porticos to passers-by, whereas the university buildings positioned on the historic "Horseshoe" face inward, looking at each other.

For a teacher of rhetoric and composition, the loud and immediate presence of state government and students' familiarity with it provides an endless rhetorical resource, a great hothouse of oral discourse. The issues the legislators tried to deal with during recent sessions were framed in the strongest symbolic terms and played out with emotional intensity; among them the flying of the Confederate flag over the State House, the exclusion of women from the state-supported military academy, the Citadel, and the bitterly contested reapportionment of legislative districts. Arguments over race, gender, history, and equality of representation have all illustrated the profoundly rhetorical nature of public discourse and underlined the rhetorical construction of public life. Yet these issues have captured the front pages precisely because of their rhetorical appeal and emotional resonance. While a few legislators, usually the same ones, are being quoted, hundreds of state employees are quietly producing memos, minutes, letters, position papers, grants, proposals, policies, regulations, annual reports, and drafts of bills and amendments as they go about the day-to-day business of state government.

Everyone knows our government is tripartite, with executive, legislative, and judicial branches. But perhaps only state employees understand the vast territory where the laws passed by legislative bodies make actual contact with citizens; this is the land of state agencies, boards, commissions, departments, and committees; the land of policy, licensing, regulation, collection, and expenditure. And this is the country that always seems to get larger and more complicated. (A few years ago when the Governor decided to reorganize the state government, no one could even agree on how many state agencies there were; counts ranged from 130 to 240, depending on what got counted.) South Carolina, a small state of 4 million people, now has about 70,000 state employees, most of whom spend their working lives producing texts. If all the state employees in all the 50 states were added together, even a conservative estimate would suggest that agency writers must number in the millions.

Agency writers write not only for the governor, the legislature, and the judiciary; they also write about education and health and social and rehabilitative services; they write about correction and conservation and transportation. And they write a great deal about regulation and licensing—from architects and auctioneers to harbor pilots and hearing-aid specialists to soil classifiers and veterinarians. They produce the annual reports often required by their enabling legislation, and they also produce texts in a vast range of contexts for a wide variety of purposes and audiences.

Such publications don't appear on best seller lists or even in bookstores, so the quantity and the variety of texts produced by state government remains largely invisible. They are all collected and housed according to their own cataloguing system in the South Carolina State Library, however, and a few years ago the librarian in charge of the collection began an awards list to draw some attention to them. Each year in commemoration of Freedom of Information Day (March 16), a small committee of librarians selects ten "Most Notable State Government Publications" that they believe "are representative of the wide-ranging functions state agencies perform and exemplify the everyday usefulness of government publications." Among the notables for

1990 were: *A Decade In Review and Issues for the 1990s: A Report on the Health and Environment of South Carolina* from the Department of Health and Environmental Control; *A Consumer's Guide to Long Term Care Insurance in South Carolina* from the Joint Legislative Committee on Aging; *Finding the Falls: A Guide to Twenty-five of the Upstate's Outstanding Waterfalls* from the Wildlife and Marine Resources Department; *Relic of the Lost Cause: The Story of South Carolina's Ordinance of Secession* from the Department of Archives and History (a 12" by 14" facsimile in a presentation folder is available for $2.00); and *Beginning a Bed and Breakfast in South Carolina: Guidelines for Development* from the Department of Parks, Recreation and Tourism.

Subsequent lists contain equally diverse items, from a film production manual, a teen pregnancy report, and a legal overview of foreign business to a bibliography of South Carolina archaeology, a report on prison crowding, and a pamphlet on minerals and rocks along with a container of sample specimens. Of course, most agency publications are not notable but routine: the Coastal Council distributes a brochure, "How to Build a Dune"; the State Museum Commission publishes its own newsletter, *Good Muse*; the Office of the State Treasurer produces *Local Government Debt Report*; the Election Commission is responsible for *Poll Manager's Handbook*; the Migrant Farm Workers Commission produces the *South Carolina Migrant Services Booklet* in English and Spanish; the State Law Enforcement Division compiles *Crime in South Carolina*; and the South Carolina State Tax Commission has its own periodical, *The Tax Commission Times-Newsletter*. The larger state agencies have their own in-house print shops; some even have art, graphics, and photography departments.

Clearly, in every state in the union, the processes of government require more writing by more writers than even writing teachers can imagine. Few who enter this world realize that whatever their agency or responsibility, most of their time will be spent writing. And few have any rhetorical training, though rhetoric—deliberative and forensic and epideictic—is inevitably what they produce. Here is where the symbiosis between state government and the university breaks down, at least to the extent that the English department has abandoned its role as purveyor of rhetorical knowledge and educator of citizens prepared for public discourse. Perhaps this is one of the reasons why agency writers discover, not only the centrality of writing in their work lives, but also this terrible truth: Of all the scribblers in the world of words, agency writers have the worst reputations. (That is why the awards list of "Notable Publications" has caused such a stir; those who win call the State Library and ask for certificates suitable for framing.)

Who would disagree that bureaucrats write the worst prose on earth? They are accused of egregious errors in spelling, punctuation, grammar and mechanics; of overburdening their sentences with pompous and inflated

language, excessive prepositional phrases, and redundancies; of hiding behind the passive, torturing their syntax, turning verbs into nouns and stringing
them together; of being disorganized, unstructured, obfuscatory, legalistic,
intentionally unclear, inchoate, and verbose.

Is agency writing as bad as its reputation? Or is it convenient and satisfying
for academics to point to a group of writers more abstruse and long-winded
than themselves? Do academics like to study bad government writing more
than they like to study and ridicule bad academic writing? Have they in fact
ever studied it? Or do they just pass along myths? Because the degree of
badness of agency writing can never be determined—even if a truly representative sample could be assembled, we could neither read it all nor agree
on what standards to apply—we are all free to go on denigrating it.

Why does agency writing have such a bad reputation? Many with whom
I spoke said, quite simply, because it *is* so bad. The director of staff development and training for the Division of Human Resource Management,
Karen Kuehner, hears agency directors complain about the writing of their
employees and hires private consultants to provide writing workshops
throughout the year. Kuehner, however, doesn't see how a workshop or
two can do much good. "Why do we even bother? By the time you're 40,
it's pretty hard to learn a different style of communication."

The more cynical believe that agency writers proceed according to an
internal code of behavior: to obfuscate. Thus, playing it safe and hiding
from blame are simply a way of life for civil servants. Agency writers themselves tend to believe that bad writing follows at least partly from the complexity of their writing tasks. Regulations about the disposal of hazardous
waste, for example, can only be highly technical, labored by virtue of the
requirements of precision and legality, inevitably long and tedious. Some
agency writers believe in a generational difference; older writers are more
formal, more likely to use legalese, less anxious to be user-friendly, more
resistant to stylistic change. Many critics suggest that the worst sins of agency
writing follow from the urge to impress an audience of superiors.

Yet somehow, in spite of all the obfuscation insiders and outsiders believe
constitutes "governmentese," laws do get written and amended, passed and
codified, applied and enforced and publicized—and all by way of texts.
Before writing teachers conclude that the writing produced by state employees is characteristically bad, they might do well to acquaint themselves with
some of the settlements in this large and complex textual territory.

LEGISLATION AS TEXT

On the second floor of the South Carolina State House in what used to be
a ballroom, the Legislative Council now performs its endless tasks. The
Legislative Council is a state agency whose mission statement reads: "The

council is responsible for the organization and operation of the research, reference, and bill drafting facilities provided to serve the General Assembly." In their cubicles (the ballroom has been partitioned to discourage eavesdropping) seven staff attorneys meet with legislators who want to introduce bills. The impetus for legislation comes from all kinds of sources—newspaper editorials, special interest groups, constituents, sometimes even "60 Minutes." The lawyer/drafters work with the House member or Senator or with designated constituents or lobbyists to frame the desired legislation. Drafted bills are worked over by standing committees, are debated and amended, and often go through as many as 15 drafts before finally being voted into law. Of course, most of the bills drafted—perhaps nine out of ten—are never passed. As the drafters compose bills, they try for a uniform, simplified style, thanks to the efforts of the National Conference of Commissioners on Uniform State Laws. This organization issued a style sheet, "Drafting Rules for Uniform or Model Acts" (1983), which offers an admirably succinct set of instructions:

> The essentials of good bill drafting are accuracy, brevity, clarity, and simplicity. The purpose and effect of an Act should be evident from its language.
>
> Choose words that are plain and commonly understood. Use language that conveys the intended meaning to every reader. Omit unnecessary words. Use correct grammar.
>
> The principal functions of an Act are (i) to create or establish, (ii) to impose a duty or obligation, (iii) to confer a power, create a right, or grant a privilege, and (iv) to prohibit. An Act is often subject to conditions, qualifications, limitations, or exceptions. The clarity and precision of the Act is enhanced by a plain and orderly expression of those functions.

Twenty-eight drafting rules follow, as well as a sample form to use for writing the sections of an Act and an appendix that bans the redundant couplets of traditional legalese (e.g., alter and change, authorize and empower, full and complete, sole and exclusive) as well as indefinite words (e.g., aforementioned, hereinafter, heretofore, therewith, wheresoever). The style sheet concludes with two columns of commands, "Do Not Say" and "Say"; here usages to be avoided are paired with preferred terms. Thus, "in the event that" becomes "if," "is authorized and directed" becomes "shall," and "it shall be lawful to" becomes "may."

The writers responsible for drafting bills are committed to simplifying the language of the laws that make their way into the code books, so they work to eliminate the "aforementioned" and "hereinafter" of old-fashioned legal writing, avoiding Latin terms whenever possible, and generally making legislation more user-friendly. David Williams, the lawyer who explained the process to me, credited law schools with initiating the move to simpler, more direct, more precise language.

The constraints the bill drafters work under seem complex to an outsider; wrestling with language to achieve clarity and precision, anticipating all possible interpretations and applications, and speaking with a uniform and authoritative voice makes writing a single sentence seem a daunting task. And the sentences of bills often must be written under extraordinary time pressures; when an amendment is proposed from the floor, staff members drop whatever they are working on and immediately start drafting. Of course, most of their sentences die as unpassed legislation. A recent bill to enable local governments to consolidate went through ten drafts as legislators tried to come up with a uniform set of procedures, then the bill failed to pass. But, said Williams, the system works, though sometimes with agonizing slowness. Some legislators have thin files of legislative activity, spending their time not introducing bills but preventing "bad" bills from becoming law; that too is part of the process.

After the 5-month legislative session is over, Williams and his colleagues spend the rest of the year summarizing new laws for publication in the *State Register*, preparing them for publication in the *Cumulative Supplement to the South Carolina Code of Laws, 1976*, and using up the compensation time they have accumulated for their long hours during the session.

The legislative process itself generates pages and pages of text as lawmakers and other state officials must be kept up-to-date on what has happened and what will happen. To that end, the Office of Research of the House of Representatives publishes a weekly newsletter (circulation 550), *Legislative Update*, during the session. Here are three paragraphs from "House Week in Review" from the 17 May 1994 issue:

> Several controversial issues took up much of the House's time this past week. The House spent much of Tuesday afternoon debating whether to give third reading to S. 920, a bill tightening requirements for land to be taxed as agricultural. Opponents made a last-ditch effort to derail the bill, warning it would lead to large tax increases for many people least able to afford them. A motion to recommit the bill to the House Agriculture, Natural Resources and Environmental Affairs Committee was tabled by a vote of 61 to 44. Also defeated was a motion to recommit the bill to the House Ways and Means Committee. S. 920 subsequently was given third reading.
>
> The issue of property tax relief resurfaced on Tuesday, when an amendment was offered to S. 674 for that purpose. The amendment would have raised the state sales tax from 5 to 7 percent, with the proceeds from this new tax used to eliminate school property taxes. The amendment also would have removed the $300 sales tax cap on the sale and lease of motor vehicles, instead imposing a 3 percent tax on those sales and leases, and would have removed approximately two-thirds of the state's 47 sales tax exemptions (including, among others, the sales tax exemption on newspapers, fuel sold to manufacturers and electric power companies for various purposes, heating material used for residential purposes, and supplies sold to radio and television

stations). The amendment, however, was ruled out of order by the Speaker. (A related but somewhat different bill to provide property tax relief, H. 5085, is still pending in the House Ways and Means Committee.)

Following approval of S. 920 late Tuesday afternoon, the House by special order then took up S. 88, a bill to regulate abortion clinics. An amendment was proposed to S. 88 which would include the "Woman's Right to Know" bill (H. 3267), requiring information be offered to women seeking abortions and also requiring a waiting period before the procedure is performed. (H. 3267 was passed by the House in early March of this year and subsequently sent to the Senate, but the bill has remained stalled in the Senate Medical Affairs Committee.) The amendment was easily adopted. Numerous amendments offered to the bill to eliminate completely the waiting period, suspend it in emergency situations, or otherwise amend it were tabled. The bill received second reading by the House that day and a perfunctory third reading the following morning. (2)

Reading *Legislative Update* very rapidly week after week, I have been struck by the clarity of the writing; the writer is able to make me understand proposed legislation, however complex, to stand back and give me a sense of what went on in the House during the week, to provide signposts, white space, and structure. One writer, a young man named Daniel O'Connor, produces this newsletter, which is sometimes as long as 50 pages. As soon as House bills are filed at the beginning of the legislative session, they are typed into the on-line computer system, the "Bill History and Status" database, in the State House. O'Connor starts in at once, summarizing each bill, for inclusion in *Legislative Update.* He will keep track of each one throughout the legislative session. On the wall beside his desk is a speaker he can switch on to either the House or the Senate to listen in to live debate; so when he writes that the House was deadlocked or the issue is volatile, he has been listening. He works long hours during the session, sometimes until 1 A.M. and most weekends. "People think I have a nine to five job, but I don't." He said that having all the bills on the network made it much easier for bills to be amended—though to Williams, the bill drafter, those amendments are on-going crises. While O'Connor is working day after day summarizing and tracking legislation, Williams is unaware of his work. State government, one soon discovers, folds back upon itself again and again, with many agency writers writing again what other writers have already written.

When the House is in session, at the end of each day a *House Journal,* which includes all of the day's happenings and any formal speeches, is published along with the *House Calendar* for the next day. These two publications, which can run to many pages, are published nightly by grave-yard shifts of computer specialists. Hanging around state government, like hanging around a newsroom, provides a writing teacher with a reminder of the speed with which writing in the nonacademic world is often produced.

LEGISLATION GENERATES TEXTS

The legislative process itself spawns pages of texts, sometimes in the thousands, for one bill. The Restructuring Bill in its final form ran to 1,816 pages. But this is only the beginning. An interesting research project would be to track the texts, their genres and authors and audiences, that are generated by a single, seemingly simple, piece of legislation. Take, for example, the bill referred to in the *Legislative Update*, House Bill 3267, "Woman's Right to Know." This bill requires that information be given to each woman seeking an abortion. The employees at the Department of Health and Environmental Control (DHEC) are well aware of what is meant here by information, because as soon the Governor signs this bill into law, it will be their job to immediately prepare and distribute to abortion clinics the five sets of documents each woman is to read before having an abortion. These include (a) a geographically indexed list of social services available for children from birth through the age of dependency; (b) a description of fetal development at two week intervals; (c) a description of the abortion procedure and the risks associated with childbirth; (d) financial support available for children; and (e) procedures for getting fathers to help support children. This mandated writing assignment is neither small nor simple—nor funded.

But DHEC is used to complex writing tasks. The health part of their enabling legislation, according to *The Code of Laws of South Carolina, Title 44, Health*, 44-1-40, seems simple and straightforward: "The Department of Health and Environmental Control may promulgate and enforce rules and regulations for public health." Such "regulations"—shortened by all insiders to "regs"—constitute the means by which legislation is translated into policies, procedures, definitions, rules, and ultimately behaviors. Regulations require an additional set of thick volumes that accompany the *Code of Laws* and that, like the Code, must be supplemented each year. Consider the regs "For the production, storing, labeling, transportation and selling of milk and milk products, filled milk and filled milk products, imitation milk and imitation milk products, synthetic milk and synthetic milk products, milk derivatives and any other products made in semblance of milk or milk products." Pages of definitions of terms are followed by pages of standards, for example, "Nonfat yogurt is the food produced by culturing one or more of the optional dairy ingredients specified in paragraph c of this section with a characterizing bacterial culture that contains the lactic acid-producing bacteria, Lactobacillus bulgaricus and streptococcus thermophilas." *Binder 24 A; Regulations: Milk and Milk Products* contains 181 pages of milk regs with another 70 pages in the supplemental volume. As I read through them, fascinated by the thoroughness, completeness, and complexity of the specifications for producing, handling, processing, and distributing milk, it gradually dawned on me: these regs are the reason I can reach for a gallon of milk in the dairy case and never worry about its quality.

Being responsible for both public health and the quality of the environment means that DHEC probably produces more regs and more technically and legally complex regs, than any other agency. But of course regulations are only one genre of the agency's writing. All of the rules and regulations must be "promulgated" by way of fact sheets, news releases, issue papers, manuals, orders, brochures, newsletters (among them, *NewsLeak*, from the Bureau of Drinking Water Protection, and *Turning the Tide*, on Nonpoint Source Water Pollution), booklets, and reports; from one-page fliers to 150-page booklets, their in-house printing operation produces over 1,500 publications a year. DHEC's Director of External Affairs, Jerry Dell Gimarc, takes pride in the range, complexity, and quality of their publications. I was struck by the attractiveness and readability of their documents as well as by the sensitivity of these agency writers to the needs of their various audiences. Gimarc prefers to hire professional journalists for permanent staff positions; potential employees submit writing samples and respond to an on-the-spot writing task. For big projects—which have made the Notable lists—she often contracts with free lance writers.

A recent publication, *Small Quantity Generator Manual : A Step by Step Manual for Businesses That Generate Small Amounts of Hazardous Waste*, could win a prize for clarity, readability, and effective graphics. Here complex technical regulations are made sensible, understandable, and doable for their intended audience (see Fig. 2.1).

Some of DHEC's writing is essentially persuasive in its aim and unashamedly emotional in its appeal. *Closing the Gap: A Call To Action, Recommendations of the South Carolina Task Force on Minority Health 1990* uses as chapter dividers these three fictional vignettes:

Mary
She could have been . . .
a teacher,
a dentist,
an astronaut,
a loving wife
and mother.

Although Mary's mother knew
to see a doctor early,
she could get cocaine easier
than prenatal care.

At birth,
Mary weighed a pound and a half.
She suffered
from cocaine addiction
and brain damage.
She could have done a lot of things,

DETERMINING YOUR GENERATOR STATUS

Refer to the S.C. Hazardous Waste Regs (R.61-79.262.34)

GENERATOR CATEGORY IS DETERMINED BY:

- The volume of hazardous waste produced per month, OR
- The volume of hazardous waste stored on-site at any one time.

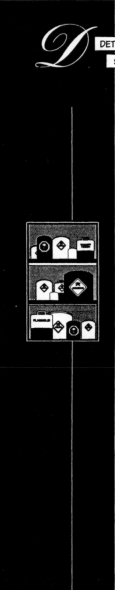

It is the responsibility of the business to determine if the waste it generates is hazardous and to determine the exact quantity generated. Some businesses that generate hazardous waste don't believe they do because they don't have a large industrial manufacturing process. However, hazardous waste may be generated in other ways as well, for example:

- If a material has been used and is spent, such as a used solvent, OR

- A stored material has exceeded its shelf life, is no longer usable and must be disposed of.

For example, a construction company or home builder may not generate the kinds of waste found in industrial processes, but it may generate hazardous waste in the form of discarded paints (sludges), solvents or other materials. Thus it would meet the classification of a hazardous waste generator.

> Because the regulations for each of the generator categories are different, it is important to determine the amount of hazardous waste you generate each month. You should also be aware of the requirements for the other categories of waste generators and how any changes in the quantity you generate will affect your regulatory requirements.

YOU MUST MEASURE OR COUNT the amount of hazardous waste you generate each month. You must add up all the weight of all the hazardous waste your business generates during a month. This total will determine your generator category.

9

■ You **do** count listed and characteristic wastes that you package for transport off-site, place in an on-site treatment or disposal unit (which must be permitted under the Resource Conservation & Recovery Act (RCRA), generate as still bottoms or sludge and remove from product storage tanks.

■ You **do not** count waste that is exempted such as used lead-acid batteries that will be reclaimed. If you are a recycling facility that stores lead-acid batteries for on-site reclamation, you do have to meet the notification of regulated waste requirements and pertinent S.C. Hazardous Waste Regs (R.61-79.266 subparts A-L) .

■ You **do not** count used oil that has been refined from crude oil, used, and as a result of such use is contaminated by physical and chemical impurities. This, of course, does not include used oil that has any listed or characteristic hazardous waste constituents. For information on used oil burned for energy recovery see S.C. Hazardous Waste Regs (R.61-79.266 subpart E) .

■ You **do not** count waste that is reclaimed continuously on-site without storing the waste before reclamation.

■ You **do not** count waste you manage in a neutralization unit. A neutralization unit may be defined as a tank, container, or transport vehicle. This unit may not have to be permitted if you maintain your conditionally exempt status (see next page), provided that it meets certain requirements. S.C. Hazardous Waste Regs (R.61-79.261.5 g3).

■ You **do not** count waste contained in a wastewater treatment unit or waste discharged to a wastewater treatment plant. This discharge must be permitted by S.C. DHEC, Bureau of Water Pollution Control, and comply with the state Pollution Control Act.

■ You **do not** count recyclable materials that may be economically utilized for precious metal recovery. However, regulations state that documentation must be kept to show the materials' intended use. This documentation should include records showing the volume of the material stored at the beginning of each calendar year. The amount of these materials generated or received during the calendar year should be included. The amount of material remaining at the end of the year should be included. These recyclable materials are subject to all applicable provisions of parts 262 through 265 and 270 when waste are accumulated speculatively. The metals included in this category are gold, silver, platinum, palladium, iridium, osmium, rhodium, ruthenium, or any combination of these.

[1 Barrel = 55 Gallons = 458 Pounds of Water = 200 Kilograms]

10

FIG. 2.1. Two sample pages from *Small Quantity Generator Manual: A Step by Step Manual for Businesses That Generate Small Amounts of Hazardous Waste*. Reprinted with permission of South Carolina Department of Health and Environmental Control.

but her life
was ruined before it began.
**Mary died at age 23 hours
of cardiovascular and
respiratory failure.**

Annette
Homemaker,
church leader,
community sparkplug,
and friend . . .
She could really
make things happen.

Someone who always
gave advice,
kept the kids,
and lent an ear.
She got her friends
to quit smoking—
But not her husband.
His cigarette habit and her
high blood pressure were
a lethal combination.
**Lung cancer caused by
second-hand smoke killed
her at 41 years.**

Raymond
Fake right, then left,
Dribble, drive,
dunk, and swish!
It was all over,
but the shouting.
And Cassandra
cheering in the stands.
Used to be
basketball was IT.

But lately, school
was good too.
Academically talented,
they said . . . And
there was money!
He had just started aiming beyond
the basketball goal
when some drughead
demanded his Nikes.
Raymond was shot

**at close range and
died instantly at age 16.**

Such writing hardly fits the stereotype of bureaucratic prose and suggests that before we draw blanket conclusions about the quality of agency writing and before we reproduce canned examples of "bureaucratese," we would do well to survey the types and kinds of documents produced by a large agency with a complex mission. As DHEC's art director said to me, "People think DHEC is a monster, but we keep your air clean and your water safe." Such assignments, which are largely carried out through texts, are neither simple nor singular.

In fact, keeping water safe is currently generating new texts in every state. In 1986, the U.S. Congress amended the Safe Drinking Water Act, increasing the number of contaminants to be regulated from 26 to over 200. Now the federal regulations—notoriously impenetrable—sent down from the Environmental Protection Agency must be written into the state regulations. The Bureau of Drinking Water Control, in the Division of Environmental Quality Control, in the Department of Health and Environmental Control is also revising the regulations for issuing permits to water treatment facilities. Regulations must be revised as technology changes, and the revision process is complex. Three engineers, an editor, and an attorney will work on this revision; the draft finally approved by the commissioners will contain all of the old language crossed out with all of the new language underlined. Then the new version will be published in the *State Register*, and public hearings will be held. In addition, the Administrative Procedures Act gives standing committees of the state legislature the authority to reject regulations. But finally, the revised regulations will be published in the *South Carolina Code of Laws*. Getting it right requires proofreading, again and again, because a misplaced comma can change the law. Defining a public water system as "15 or more taps or 25 or more people served 60 days out of the year," means something different from "15 or more taps or 25 or more people, served 60 days out of the year." These writers know that not getting it right will have consequences.

Some state agencies exist only to produce writing. The Legislative Audit Council, a watchdog agency mandated to perform "independent, objective performance audits of state operations" for the legislature, reviews the performance of other agencies in terms of economy, efficiency, and compliance. Staff members, called auditors, do nothing but produce reports, and they are highly self-critical of the readability of their products. (See Magnotto's chapter, this volume, on government evaluators at the federal level.) Their report-writing procedure could provide an interesting context for a case study of collaborative writing. Each project the council undertakes is assigned to a team that develops an audit plan; the plan is divided up and each team member is assigned an area on which to research and report. After their field work, and lengthy scrutiny of all the relevant documents of the agency or program they are auditing, they write up preliminary reports. Then the editing and re-editing begins, as team members exchange reports, suggest changes, meet, and meet again. Pride of authorship—exactly what we try to instill in our student writers—must be abandoned in favor of a uniform agency voice and must be subordinated to the hierarchical structure of the agency. The senior auditor rules the audit team, the audit manager rules the senior auditor, the director of the agency rules the senior auditor, and the director is responsible to the members of the council. Such a stack of bureaucrats might suggest considerable indirection and covering of bases. But, in fact, the publications of the Legislative Audit Council are direct and hard-hitting. See, for example, the summary from their report, *A Management Review of the Savannah Valley Authority* (Fig. 2.2).

This piece of writing—clear, direct, and accusatory—can hardly be considered obfuscatory or agentless. In fact, like the style of bill-writing, the style and presentation of the council's reports have undergone a dramatic change in the last several years. They are now produced with sophisticated graphics, subheads, and white space and are written in a journalistic style that is determinedly reader-friendly. The agency refers to itself in the first person plural, which makes for agent-action-goal sentences as opposed to passive constructions. Their final product, a published and bound report, now contains a one-page, pull-out summary so that legislators can get the substance of the entire report quickly. And yet, the Legislative Audit Council's style, which seems to follow all of the precepts of writing teachers, has its critics. The director of another agency told me that the audit council's reports were "straight jacketed" by this style, which leads to overstatement and sweeps of logic; sentences quoted out of context can be unfairly damning, lacking in nuance and complexity, and politically dangerous. Thus, the style that an agency adopts should be understood as a complicated matter; following the rules of a style book may or may not yield an effective political agenda. Sometimes hedging is ethical.

Because state government, like any species, likes to duplicate itself, another agency, the Reorganization Commission, writes its own reports on the reports of the Legislative Audit Council. Thus, an Act creates an agency, which eventually requires another agency to audit it, and a further agency to audit the auditors, and, in this way, texts multiply. At least that is how the documents produced by these two agencies look to an outsider. But there is usually a reason for duplicated efforts. When I talked to an insider, I learned that the function of the Reorganization Commission is to take the objective, apolitical appraisals of the Legislative Action Council and put them into play in the political arena. Thus, the findings of an audit can be acted upon, but not by the auditors, who need to maintain their outsider stance. To be useful as a writing consultant in state government means spending a good bit of time learning the real rules of the game, as well as the stated ones.

THE NEW ETHOS OF AGENCY COMMUNICATION

Some state agencies operate primarily within state government, creating documents that will be read only by other insiders. The style of these internal texts is likely to assume an insider audience, to be laden with special terms, to be stiffer and more "bureaucratic." But, according to Philip Grose, Director of the Executive Institute, most state agencies and most enlightened agency directors know that their power comes from dealing effectively and openly with three points of power: the legislature, the press, and the public. This has not always been the case. Formerly, civil servants could operate behind closed doors; running their organizations, complying with the law, and spending appropriations was good enough for many—and nobody's business. Then there was Watergate, and the subsequent passing of "sunshine laws" or Freedom of Information Acts in state after state, asserting the public's right to know.

Now agencies must conduct their business more openly, must be accountable, must interact positively with their constituencies. Elected and appointed officials who won't talk to the press are learning that whatever press they have is likely to be a bad one. Of course, different states have very different Freedom of Information laws. In South Carolina, a polite and conservative place, state salaries below the $50,000 range are considered private matters, and discussions of personnel matters can be conducted "in executive session." (Executive sessions are convenient for throwing out reporters; the entire state Senate can go into executive session if it chooses, and it often does.) What is rude in one part of the country is a citizen's right to know in another, but all over the country, state agencies have undergone a sea change, from business behind closed doors to the public's right to information. Large state agencies have public relations departments, research and communications divisions, public information directors, media relations specialists, and even TV production studios. These jobs are likely to be filled by experienced reporters—perhaps tired of the pace of the newsroom—who bring their journalistic skills to agency affairs. When a big, important project needs to be produced, free lance writers are often hired. Creating documents that are both attractive and readable has become a high priority—higher it would seem in agencies than in academies.

Not every agency writer went to journalism school, however. Among those 70,000 state employees, there are terrible writers who prove our worst imaginings, producing impenetrable prose, uninterpretable laws, and unreadable sentences. But some insiders find old style bureaucratese less of-

Briefing Report to the General Assembly

LAC

September 1993

A Management
Review of the
Savannah Valley Authority

Members of the General Assembly requested that we conduct a performance audit of the Savannah Valley Authority (SVA). Our review focused on the agency's management from FY 90-91 through the spring of 1993. The mission of the SVA, located in McCormick, was to promote economic development in the 13 counties of the Savannah River basin. On July 1, 1993, the authority became the Division of Savannah Valley Development of the Department of Commerce.

We reviewed the contracts and projects administered by the SVA and found that the authority did not hold its contractors and other entities accountable for the results of state expenditures. We found evidence that the SVA did not exercise adequate oversight in its use of state resources.

Savannah Valley Authority 13-County Jurisdiction

NORTH CAROLINA

SOUTH CAROLINA

GEORGIA

ATLANTIC
OCEAN

Contract Management

We identified several problems with the authority's contract with The Fontaine Company, Inc. (p. 7). The SVA paid this consultant more than $2 million in fees and expenses for work beginning in December 1990 and ending in May 1993. We found that:

●The contract gave The Fontaine Company sole discretion in assigning employees to tasks, and 83% of the fees charged were at the highest rate of $150 per hour. Senior-level employees performed such tasks as collecting names and addresses of hunters.

●The contract did not have an overall budget, and there were no caps or limits to the amount of money to be paid for Fontaine's services.

●The contract lacked any provision requiring that services be completed, although such a provision is required by law. Many of the services required by the contract were not completed and did not result in an identifiable product or outcome for the authority.

●The SVA director did not establish procedures to authorize Fontaine's work or monitor costs. The SVA paid for work that appeared unnecessary; for example, it spent approximately $111,000 for demographic and economic data about the town of Calhoun Falls, which has a population of only 2,328.

▶

South Carolina Legislative Audit Council ■ 400 Gervais St. ■ Columbia, SC 29201 ■ (803)253-7612

48

Amounts Spent on Lobbying

We reviewed the authority's expenditures for lobbying from December 1990 through March 1993 (p. 16). The SVA paid about $155,500 in fees and expenses for consultants to lobby state government and about $169,500 for consultants to lobby federal officials. For FY 91-92, lobbying accounted for 10% of the SVA's expenditures. The authority underreported the amount it spent to lobby state government by more than $91,000 in a 15-month period.

Computer Model Funding

The SVA did not exercise appropriate controls over the $385,000 it paid the Water Resources Commission to develop a computer model of the Savannah River lake system (p. 21). There was no written agreement between the SVA and water resources which defined each agency's responsibility for funding or ensured that the product would be completed.

Lake Russell Project Management

We reviewed the management of the Lake Richard B. Russell project on 3,300 acres adjacent to Lake Russell and the town of Calhoun Falls (p. 29). This project is still in the planning stages. We found the following problems:

- The SVA did not require The Fontaine Company to complete a project implementation plan for the Lake Russell site, as required by contract.

- A proposal for a 100-room lodge and recreational complex is the major product of the $1.5 million paid to Fontaine for this project. This strategy of focusing on the lodge was based on the SVA's need for income, not on an overall development plan.

- The SVA plan focused on the use of state funds to build the lodge, instead of private development funds. This would put state funds at risk if the venture were unsuccessful.

Aiken County Project Management

We also reviewed the SVA's use of $4.5 million in capital improvement bonds that were authorized in 1991 for an "Aiken County project" (p. 33). We found the authority to be in compliance with the legislative mandate and state procedural requirements. However, we identified some problems with SVA's management of one proposed commitment of the bond funds:

- A proposed commitment of $3.5 million to a start-up company to locate in Aiken County ended in a contractual dispute and a $50,000 settlement paid by the SVA. We did not find adequate evidence of board authorization for SVA's actions regarding the commitment and settlement.

- The executive director permitted The Fontaine Company to deviate from its written contract by allowing a contingency pay arrangement instead of payment on an hourly basis.

Savannah Lakes Village

Savannah Lakes Village was the authority's first major development project, undertaken jointly with a private development company, Cooper Communities, Inc., beginning in 1988 (p. 37). We reviewed selected management issues related to Savannah Lakes Village:

- We reviewed a $20 million loan from the Insurance Reserve Fund to finance infrastructure for the development. We found that the special tax paid by the development's residents should be adequate to meet the debt service schedule (p. 38).

- We reviewed changes to the agreements governing the development and concluded the changes should have no detrimental effect on the state's or SVA's interest in the project. However, we could find no evidence that SVA's board approved some of the changes (p. 41).

We also identified problems with the authority's internal management of personnel, accounting, vehicles and equipment (pp. 23-26).

Responses to our audit begin on page 47.

South Carolina Legislative Audit Council ■ 400 Gervais St. ■ Columbia, SC 29201 ■ (803)253-7612

FIG. 2.2. Legislative Audit Council briefing report. Reprinted with permission of South Carolina Legislative Audit Council.

fensive than new style excesses of sensibility, such as "Let me share with
you . . ."

Uncovering the ethos of an agency as well as collecting the documents
it typically produces is part of the homework required for effective consulting.

A WRITING TEACHER IN A STATE AGENCY

My own introduction to and interest in the process of state government
began in 1985 when Governor Richard Riley (President Clinton's Secretary
of Education) appointed me to the South Carolina Commission on Women.
This state agency, a very small one, was created in 1971 to demonstrate a
commitment to improving the status of women. In fact, it was originally
called the Commission on the Status of Women; but after a lawsuit brought
by a private citizen charging that the Commission was in fact lobbying for
the Equal Rights Amendment (ERA), the enabling legislation was rewritten
and the Commission renamed. Now the Commission's mandate is to report
to the governor with recommendations on the concerns of women; to research, study, and disseminate information on women's issues; to receive
and disburse state and federal grants—but *not* to lobby for the ERA, or any
ERA, ever. We are about the smallest state agency and we have one of the
tiniest budgets—even the appropriation for the Commission on Migratory
Wildfowl is larger than our paltry $80,000—and, as we have been heard to
complain, their constituents are not even South Carolina residents.

The formation of the Commission on Women could be seen, by the
cynical, as one of Foucault's dividing practices, whereby a group is separated
and labeled in order to be controlled, in this case, ignored. The Commission
on Women has been given just enough money to exist, but not really enough
to accomplish anything; just enough recognition for some committed women
to try hard, burn out, and move on without gaining much ground. Nevertheless, in genteel poverty the SCCW tries to lead an agency life, though
sometimes our executive director has to cut back to work ¾ time in order
to reserve enough of the budget to pay her two assistants, both of whom
are part time.

For 8 years I served on the Commission and was chair for three of those
years. As chair of the Commission, I became, for the first time, a participant
in the discourse of public administration, of the legislative process, of the
executive office, of partisan politics, of the popular media, of women's
networks and coalitions, and of individual women with questions, complaints, and problems. And the experience made me realize how academic,
abstract, optimistic, other-worldly, literary, and individualistic are most of
our communication models—especially as they attempt to explain the con-

cept of audience. (I used to muse on this as I left the Commission office, where I signed letters I had not written, and entered my university classroom, where I talked to students about ownership of their texts.)

Certainly, in thinking about how writing gets accomplished and how it accomplishes, we have made some theoretical progress. We have gotten beyond the linear notion of the writer implanting meaning in a text for the reader to extract. Now we allow that the writer constructs meaning and discovers purpose by the act of writing and that the reader participates as co-producer of the text. But both poststructuralist and social constructionist models, however complex their explanation of audience, still tend to assume a single writer as the locus of text production. This is a very literary attitude—as Foucault has shown us, "literary discourses came to be accepted only when endowed with the author function"—and one almost impossible to think against given the reigning academic conditions for writing: student to teacher or scholar to scholarly audience (109). Linda Brodkey calls it the scene of writing, alone in the garret with a candle.

But as we have seen, agencies themselves are authors. The Legislative Council authors legislation, the Legislative Audit Council authors audits, the Department of Health and Environmental Control authors regulations. The South Carolina Commission on Women is largely "an author" because much if not most of its time is spent producing documents. Our newsletter (before it got too expensive) had a readership of 10,000; our legal brochures on "Women and Credit"; "Women, Wills, and Estates"; "Women, Marriage, and Divorce"; "Women and Property Rights" are broadly circulated; and staff members are constantly engaged in producing letters, reports, position papers, grants, press releases, and testimony. Who is this writer? It cannot, of course, be one person, but must be what Gesa Kirsch calls an interpretive framework, here a collective interpretive framework, an abstraction, which each of us entered into and committed to in spite of sometimes deep philosophical and political differences (220). We all agreed on what it means to "speak for the Commission" and in what contexts and on what issues we were empowered to do so. (Those who broke the rules were reprimanded.) This individual commitment to a collective voice which we could all speak was remarkable to me, because the party in power changed from Democratic to Republican during my tenure and since the make-up of the Commission consequently changed dramatically. We had been six Democrats and one far right Republican, appointed after the law suit; then we were five Republicans, among them a bank executive, a school teacher, a college professor, a restaurant manager, a lawyer, and two Democrats, a school administrator and a college professor. (The two Democrats managed reappointment by the Republican governor through wire pulling, wheedling, and casuistry performed by their Republican colleagues.) Furthermore, the director changed from a radical Democratic feminist with a flair for investigative journalism to a Republican wife-mother-churchwoman who planned to run for office to an art historian with a certificate in Women's Studies and family political connections in the Democratic party.

Yet, we all knew how to speak the voice so that who wrote the document was unimportant. Given our constantly changing staff (no one keeps a job that pays that little for very long), we often didn't know who wrote what. Once, for example, as I signed a letter to the governor, I praised the staff member who had written it. She said, "Oh, I copied it from last year's letter." And I realized that I had perhaps written the letter myself. "What difference does it make who is speaking?" asks Foucault at the end of "What is an Author?" (120) It made no difference to us because we agreed on how we should sound. Thus, when I asked my fellow commissioners, "If you could characterize the Commission as a person, what sort of person would you want us to be?" their answers were powerfully coherent: "Influential and effective, a caring individual that understands those different from herself, but able to function and influence those who don't care about those individuals. Knowledgeable, visible, involved, bright, tough but fair, articulate, representative of all women in the state regardless of political preference, a leader, balanced but progressive on women's issues." This is a persona we tacitly adopted, setting aside our individual causes and party affiliations though they were fairly intense—or we wouldn't have been appointed to this Commission. So, as I left that communal office where "pride of authorship" was totally inappropriate, and entered my own isolated office in a nine-story building full of prima donnas committed to lengthening their bibliographies, I was always struck by just how academic the academic world is—even the world of writing teachers. I was struck by how our endless emphasis on individuality, on the writer and the writer's voice and the writer's intentions, creations, and products is remote indeed from the reality of agency writing—which, as we have seen, thousands of civil servants spend their lives producing as they enact legislation and negotiate the social services of a democracy. (And I would hazard that more of our students will end up as agency writers than as academic ones.)

I am also struck when reading our theories by our assumption that there is always time for the time writing takes, "time for decisions and revisions," time to balance or even think about the demands of the audience addressed versus the audience invoked. Much agency life is about putting out fires, responding to crises, coming up with something because somebody needed it yesterday, meeting deadlines. Our report for the Reorganization Commission had to be ready by 3:50 P.M. because that was when our testimony was scheduled. Agency writers are great recyclers, not of paper, but of words, sentences, paragraphs, and purposes because there is never time to think it through from scratch, to follow the steps of the composing processes we teach. And there will never be time.

Nor will our documents be read slowly and carefully by those friendly and cooperative and painstaking readers who seem to inhabit textbook descriptions of audience. We do have friendly readers: the women who receive our newsletter and who call our office for information. And we do have friendly audiences, the numerous and varied women's groups who ask us for a speaker for their next meeting. But even our friends can get hostile. Young women tell us we are not being aggressive enough; older women tell us not to be obnoxious. So to stay sane, we project a large group of voiceless women for whom we imagine we speak. When I surveyed commissioners and staff about who we are speaking *for*, they agreed: "We should speak for the women who have the least"; "grassroots women, those who do not know/would not know unless we are there for them: divorce victims, teenage mothers, working women, single parents"; "We should particularly speak for those women who have difficulty to speak for themselves." These women constitute the discourse community we believe we represent, and they are in fact a collection of groups with disparate concerns, from pregnant teenagers who drop out of school, to displaced homemakers, to mothers without child support, to business women who can't get credit, to university administrators who have hit the glass ceiling. Nevertheless, these audiences are our friends, those for whom we speak.

But agencies exist in the space between citizens and government. And agency life is about bringing the needs of our constituency to the attention of those in power. It is our mission to create a space, to break into, to gain a hearing in the discourse community of power. Thus, our most important audiences are legislators, especially committee chairmen, and the governor and his staff. These audiences may be polite, but they are not friendly. They are profoundly hostile. They are especially fearful of having any of their political initiatives labeled or connected with "women's issues." Of course, foregrounding women's issues and connecting them with the realities of South Carolina's dismal statistics—the highest infant mortality rate in the nation, for example—is our mission.

Recent theories of audience, especially those that deconstruct the boundaries between writer and reader, assert that our old models assumed too much hostility, too adversarial a role between writer and reader. From the perspective of Bakhtin, for example, the self dissolves in intersubjectivity; the text dissolves in intertextuality (Phelps 162). But the reality of trying to accomplish change in the political arena is no carnival. In fact, as we prepare documents for our hostile audiences, we seldom assume enough hostility.

We did not assume enough hostility on the part of the Senate Judiciary Committee when it revised the probate code; it did not want to hear that spouses should have a right to an elective share—after all, surviving spouses tend to be women. Nor did the House Ways and Means Committee want to hear our complaints and pleadings about our embarrassingly small budget.

The State Reorganization Commission couldn't imagine that women still had problems with employment or equal pay. The State Division of Personnel was panicked when one of our interns started looking into how many women compared to how many men were employed at what levels in state government. The House Education Committee did not want to hear that women should be allowed to attend the state-supported military academy, the Citadel. Neither the House nor the Senate wanted to pass a law against marital rape. And so on.

Hostile audiences such as these are not going to "engage in a play of significations," not going to "envision alternative readings," and are not going to play the role we have written for them (Roth). We have found that their standard techniques of response are: (a) to deny that we are experts, to say our facts our wrong; (b) to insist that we are only telling the bad stories, the extremes; (c) to blame the victim—for example, women who lose custody of their children are bad mothers, women who write bad checks to buy food are really trading the milk and bread for cocaine; (d) to say thank you for your testimony; of course there is no money, but we do care; (e) to dismiss us; "Now you go back there and don't cause any trouble now," said one senator to our director.

That the world of public policy is neither polite nor welcoming compared to the world of scholarly discourse struck me powerfully when I read Berkenkotter's study, "Evolution of a Scholarly Forum: *Reader*: 1977–1988." This story of how a group of reader-response critics established for themselves a place in the discipline and defined a new territory yielded a genuine happy ending. I had to conclude that the *Reader* venture was successful because no one with any real power cared. Agency writers, in bringing the needs of their constituencies to the attention of the audience with power, confront the reality of Foucault's discursive regime. A group of almost exclusively male legislators, for example, has a real interest in not passing stiff legislation enforcing child support payments.

One of the most revealing incidents of my term as a commissioner occurred when, after two years of trying, the Commission on Women finally persuaded the Governor's scheduler to put us on his calendar, and she allowed us the Governor's lunch hour, 30 minutes. (Again, the modalities are haste and hostility, not time and cooperation.) We put together a briefing paper—in the usual rush—which outlined six recommendations for a partnership with the Governor's staff and three policy issues for developing a women's agenda. At the appointed hour we were ushered into the paneled conference room with the deep red leather chairs in the South Carolina State House, and in he came, our number one audience, the Governor. And we watched him read our text. Sitting at the head of the long mahogany table with aides running in and out carrying slips of paper, he was not "a textual entity"—as some audience theorists might have us believe (Roth 184). He was, first, a man on the defensive, no doubt nervous to even have a Commission on Women. (The boundary between audience and authorship had *not* disappeared [Phelps 159].) He had brought two aides with him (for protection): the young woman special assistant for education, whom I will call Staffer Friendly, and the businessman-turned-political appointee in charge of gubernatorial appointments, whom I will call Staffer Hostile.

The Governor read with two techniques. The first was to use our text as a take-off point for puffing his own political activities. He then had national political ambitions and had been working on a program called Caring for Tomorrow's Children, which he told us about at length. The Governor wanted us to sign on to his support for children's issues; he did not want to join us in support of women's issues. (Submerging women's issues in children's issues is a common way to "disappear" women.) His second reading technique was to find wrong information. We had brought a list of the 50 major state agencies which have 0 to 2 women members on their boards, and he pounced on some errors. However, he did talk to us seriously and at length, holding the floor, relaxing as he realized we were not on the attack. (Southern ladies do not go on the attack; in my introductory remarks I said that the Commission's relationship with the Governor was "bad" and I was immediately contradicted by a colleague. "Oh no! It's not bad," she corrected.) And he did agree to our request for a direct line of communication to his office—our primary goal—but mostly he deflected our text.

One of the reasons we had insisted on meeting with him face-to-face was to see who he really was because we had finally figured out that *sending* documents to him was a bizarre lottery that depended on who handled our text. Picture these two scenarios: The Commission on Women sends a letter of petition to the Governor, and Staffer Friendly, known to be sensitive to women's issues and known to be highly respected for her administrative skills, hands it to him or tells him about it. Or imagine that Staffer Hostile, hired to ensure doctrinal loyalty and partisan appointments, transmits our text. I submit that Staffer Hostile would not even need to roll his eyes to totally subvert our message. The Governor is of course surrounded by staffers: a chief of staff, six executive assistants, a communications director appointed to appease the far right Christian fundamentalist wing, a public relations person, and many more. Hence, when a document is sent to the Governor's office, *who* opens *what* makes all the difference. We now know that, given a particular issue, we should send a particular commissioner to a particular staff member to walk our document in. Once we figured this out, we felt awfully stupid for not having known it all along. It is so obvious—except in academic or textbook discussions of audience. The Governor, though a single individual, is not a single audience; he is a different audience for each of his staffers and has as many response modes as the political contexts in which he appears. The Commission on Women, though a multiple and constantly changing writer is steadfastly singular in its outlook, speaking for those in need to those in power. We are constantly trying to achieve "socialization" into the discourse community of power—and gaining a hearing requires more political savvy than novices can imagine (Porter 248).

We always had to anticipate hostility because we always live in the cross fire. We knew that the Commission could be eliminated at the stroke of a pen; every few years someone tries it. ("Do we have a Commission on Men?" is a question I answered again and again. "Yes. 240 of them.") We had to be very careful; we knew that some issues—like abortion—were just too hot to handle. Our official position was that we had no position; this struck me as both politically wise and a terrible cop out.

Thus, most of our recent theories about audience came to seem academic, abstract, optimistic, other-worldly, literary, and individualistic. And poststructural notions of audience—texts dissolved in intertextuality, selves submerged in intersubjectivity—became ludicrously ethereal and amorphous self-projections. Eliminating the linear or stage theory, refusing to see the writer and reader as discrete makes a lot of sense—in theory. But when the Chairman of the House Ways and Means Committee is staring you down, the boundaries feel very real. In historical time, some texts are profoundly hostile to other texts. But, everything can change in a minute. The Marital Rape bill finally passed because some of the key opponents were running for judgeships and needed positive press. And when the paper carried a story, "McAlister Named Chief of Staff in Governor's Office Reshuffling," we knew we were back at square one, figuring out who should carry in our letter. (At least I now knew enough to cut that story out, paste it on the wall, memorize the new names and titles.)

The unified voice of the Commission on Women spoke out, albeit very politely, in spite of our political differences for several years. Then one day it cracked. The issue was whether or not women should be admitted to the Citadel, whether or not the Commission should take a public stand, and whether or not we should allow ourselves to be silenced by the Governor's staff. These disagreements got ugly, and our collegial, bipartisan voice and commitment disintegrated. Such is the reality of agency life; democracy, like sausage, is not pretty in the making.

Teachers of writing need reality lessons and need ways to counterweight the inevitable academic bias of both our theories and our practice. One is to develop, promote, and stay involved with student intern programs. Interns for the Commission on Women tracked relevant legislation and reported to us, others worked on research projects and wrote opinion papers; these young women were thrust into real-world writing and given responsibilities and assignments that amazed them—and me too. Another way is to put our names in the talent bank to serve on state boards and commissions; state agencies can always use experts, and we can always use a dose of practical experience. If rhetoric teaches us anything, it is surely the overriding importance of local conditions. Learning about and engaging with our own local conditions can improve our citizenship and correct our theories. As we continue our analysis of audience, we would do well, I think, to keep in mind the words of Alexis De Tocqueville, writing on the role of literary intellectuals in the French Revolution:

> Their very way of living led these writers to indulge in abstract theories and generalizations regarding the nature of government, and to place a blind confidence in these. For living as they did, quite out of touch with practical politics, they lacked the experience which might have tempered their enthusiasms. Thus they completely failed to perceive the very real obstacles in the way of even the most praiseworthy reforms, and to gauge the perils involved in even the most salutary revolutions (140).

So for writing teachers, especially for writing teacher/consultants, keeping in touch with "practical politics" provides a healthy check on the enthusiasms of "theory."

WORKING WITH AGENCY WRITERS

My own experience as an "appointed official" gave me a necessary head start as a writing consultant within state government; I knew at least the outlines of the territory and the names of some of the residents. State personnel departments, now usually called human resources management, contract with private writing consultants to provide the types of writing instruction that agencies want or think they want. Some of these training sessions are at fairly basic levels and rely on worksheets and rule books. But agency writers at executive levels need more sophisticated writing instruction; the workshops I conduct with middle and upper level management begin with an introduction to rhetorical context.

During Clinton's presidential campaign, his political strategists kept their focus by working under a sign that read "The economy, Stupid." Agency writers would do well to make for themselves a sign reading "The audience, Stupid." A writing course for public administrators, it seems to me, must begin with a thorough grounding in the concept of audience—which, as we have seen, can be complex indeed. A lecture on audience, however, is likely to be a sleeper; the word "audience" needs unpacking to be of use. Consultants, after all, are not paid for new insights but for repackaging old ones in memorable ways. Getting agency writers to change their conceptions about what writing is and about their own writing tasks and problems requires some kind of a wake-up call. One that I have found successful is the memo written by a National Aeronautics and Space Administration (NASA) budget analyst about the erosion of O-ring seals in the rocket motors for the space shuttle Challenger. This memo, part of the public domain since Congressional hearings, is reprinted and analyzed in Herndl, Fennell, and Miller's article, "Understanding Failures in Organizational Discourse" in *Textual Dynamics of the Professions*, ed. Charles Bazerman and James Paradis (279–305). It warns of the possible failure of the seals on the O-rings during flight and says prophetically, "failure during launch would certainly be catastrophic." I ask participants in my workshops to raise their hands when they figure out what this memo is about. That they do figure it out is, of course, the point. The memo failed, not because it was badly written and unclear, but because it neglected issues outside the text—the relationship of the writer to his audience. "Writing," says my handout, "is not just what's on the page." A second memo included in Herndl, Fennell, and Miller's analysis concerns potential problems at the Three Mile Island nuclear power plant. With a few hints, participants also figure out this memo, even though they are not rocket scientists or nuclear physicists. Again, the problem is not the correctness of the text, not convoluted sentences, bad grammar, technical language, doublespeak, or any of the traditional sins of bureaucratese, but the relationship between writer and audience. In this instance, because the writer seemed to be questioning the status of a supervisor, his message was responded to as a political threat rather than as a safety issue. Agency writers are of course used to having their texts ignored or read for the wrong reasons, also with disastrous results, and these memos help them to see that the problem with failed communication—in spite of all the myths about bureaucratic writing—is usually not just textual; having the commas in the right places will not insure a document's effectiveness.

Explaining the concept of audience requires more than dramatic disasters. Writers of texts for public contexts, like all writers, need a dose of theory, a communication model of some kind that enables them to assess the rhetorical exigencies of each textual task. One that has worked well for me comes from Bogert and Worley's textbook, *Managing Business Communications* (see Fig. 2.3). This model places the entire communicative act in an Environment, "both the immediate environment and the culture as a whole" (19). As we have seen, Freedom of Information Acts have changed the culture of state agencies, just as new management philosophies have changed the environment for business communications. Bogert and Worley's model also includes the process of feedback, particularly relevant to agency writers because so many of their documents are reviewed and approved by others. Writers at DHEC put their texts on a local area network and edit each other constantly. The *State Register*, where all new regulations are first published, exists to provide the public with an opportunity for feedback. And the reports of the Legislative Audit Council are first sent to the agency being audited, which has a right as well as a

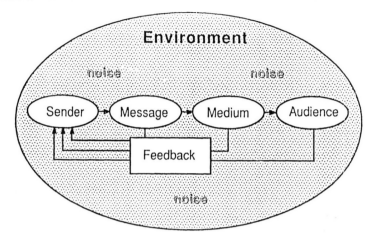

FIG. 2.3. The Communication Pathway.

responsibility to respond to the audit; their response is published in the Audit
Council's published report—so feedback is part of the public record. But the
part of the model that participants in my workshops tell me they have been
most impressed with is the gray background labeled "noise." Agency writers
may be more acutely aware of noise than the rest of us; perhaps bureaucracies
create noise as an inevitable byproduct the way other industries produce
pollutants. At any rate, the idea that a piece of communication must overcome
the existing noise—whether political or cultural—makes immediate sense.

Models need applying, and analyzing some famous and infamous historical quotations appeals to public administrators who have spent their lives
in the political arena, listening to successes and failures. If there is at least
one senior participant, I begin with Eisenhower's campaign promise, "I will
go to Korea." This sentence was not especially noteworthy stylistically but
extremely effective politically. Only Eisenhower, however, the commander
of the Normandy invasion, could have made this message work to a public
that wanted out of a war. Nixon's assertion, "I am not a crook," did not
work. For purposes of melodrama, I have always argued that this very
remark ultimately caused his downfall. His audience was watching the President of the United States in the Oval Office with the flags and the presidential
seal; hearing him use the word "crook" created a disharmony so intense
that his negation became an admission of guilt. Then there is Alexander
Haig's remark moments after the assassination attempt on Ronald Reagan,
"I am in control here at the White House." But his audience was not the
troops, but the White House press corps, experts on the line of succession,
outraged at his presumption.

Thus, some solutions to rhetorical problems are better than others. Agency
writers, tapping into their institutional memories, can recall examples of both

successful and unsuccessful solutions. They can also come up with a current rhetorical problem they need to solve. And when they do, the complexities of message and purpose, of what needs to be accomplished and what needs to be avoided, as well as the nature of the audience and the types of prevailing noise—sometimes partisan politics—become apparent. I ask them to think about one of their immediate rhetorical tasks and sketch out all of its parts: (a) the author's function in the organization, (b) the purpose of the text to be produced, (c) the immediate audience as well as other intended audiences, and (d) the constraints that will affect its production. Creating a text involves a trade-off between effectiveness (making the case thoroughly and comprehensively), and efficiency (making the case quickly and simply enough that it will be read). Solving such problems requires a process.

Writing research has shown us that lack of planning accounts for many of the problems and anxieties of writers on the job. So developing a plan while keeping the audience and purpose in mind is the essential next step, the step that, neglected, leads to chaos. Some inspirational talk is in order, here, about how planning is easier than drafting, so throwing away a bad plan is less upsetting than throwing away a bad draft; about how time spent planning is time saved; and about how we can use our minds to structure discourse while we are sitting in boring meetings, taking showers, or walking on a treadmill. Coming up with a plan for solving a real rhetorical problem and then explaining that plan to a partner requires both participants to focus on the process and to get some feedback.

Learning to structure discourse so that it both fulfills the writer's purpose and meets the needs of an audience is the hardest task for every writer. And teaching writers how to structure discourse is the hardest task for a writing teacher; that is why so many writing texts for so long have offered students formulas to fill—five-paragraph themes or good news/bad news letters—rather than necessary principles for structuring discourse. I present writers—whether in a classroom, a newsroom, or a state agency—with two structuring tools that help them understand how information can be organized and how organization can help or hinder readers.

The first is the *abstraction ladder*, that useful metaphor for the hierarchical nature of language. The abstraction ladder can be presented by way of Hayakawa's familiar cow diagram (153), the pyramidal structure of a state agency, or the levels of generality of the traditional I, II, III, A, B, C, 1, 2, 3 outline. But the truth that it uncovers remains the same: Good writing moves up and down the abstraction ladder from the abstract to the concrete and from the specific to the general. The most readable writing, such as detective fiction, stays low on the ladder, concentrating on the concrete details of corpses and weapons, exemplifying rather than explaining. Philosophical discourse stays high, offering abstract propositions and explanations. Writing that explains or convinces or informs, yet is easy on readers, moves up and down, connecting data with conclusions, propositions with support, generalizations with specifics, explanation with exemplification.

The levels of abstraction can be seen in psycholinguistic terms as well. Readers expect texts to be structured hierarchically, according to global plans that offer directions for processing the text's information. In processing a text, readers reach for abstract patterns, frames, scripts, and schemas that enable them to put a text together. But readers are impressed and surprised and interested by the concrete data, details, specifications, and visual images that enable them to construct a physical reality. It seems that readers structure texts from the top down but are affected from the bottom up. When writers understand the abstract structural needs of readers, as well as their need for actual, visual, concrete information, they understand why good writing necessarily moves up and down levels of abstraction and generality. At what level is most agency writing? The level is from high to higher, participants usually agree, just as they agree that the writers they consider the most effective are known for making readers "see." To familiarize them with switching levels, I ask them to take a statement such as "state government is inefficient" and render it more concretely, or to take their job title and explain what they really do.

Although writing teachers have been using the abstraction ladder as a teaching technique for years, we have gained new understanding of it through the work of George Lakoff in *Women, Fire, and Dangerous Things*. According to Lakoff, in every culture, we enter the world of language at the level of the general term, that is, *cow, coin, flower, dog*. Such general terms or "prototypes" are the staples of our vocabularies and of our descriptions of reality; they are the first-learned, fastest-recalled terms of our linguistic lives. When a pet unexpectedly enters a classroom, for example, observers will exclaim, "Look at the dog," not "Look at the cocker spaniel" or "Look at the mammal" (46). We are comfortable and articulate at the level of the prototype as readers of freshman essays are well aware: "In today's modern world, many people think . . ." Moving to lower levels of specificity or higher levels of abstractness requires "achievements of the imagination" (32). That is why writing is hard. We must work to get beyond generalities and to achieve structure, purpose, and effect. Understanding the hierarchical nature of language and the reasons for exploiting it, to provide structure and to be memorable, makes rhetorical success possible, explainable, and nonmystical. Effective agency writers already understand these principles. For example, the Legislative Audit Council's assertion in "A Management Review of the Savannah Valley Authority" that money had been misspent was supported by the fact of a $111,000 demographic study about a town of 2,328 people (Fig. 2.2). The DHEC poems ask us to *imagine* actual people.

Another way of explaining to writers why readers need structure is to turn to linguistic theory. The principle of relevance states that "readers try to obtain from each new item of information as great a contextual effect as possible for as small as possible processing effort" (Sperber and Wilson 141–142). The principle might be stated informally as "the biggest bang for the smallest buck." That is, readers want to be surprised by new information that might strengthen, contradict, or eliminate an existing assumption, but they want this contextual effect to happen painlessly. They want informative material in conventional structures, new wine in old bottles. Writers who understand these principles are much better equipped to organize their texts than those who are shown traditional forms for memos and reports.

A text needs an organizing principle and readers need to be cued to what that principle is. But a global plan can only be carried out locally, sentence by sentence. In writing that reads easily—transparently—the writer controls the flow of information so that readers' short-term memories are not over-taxed. *Controlling the flow of information* is the second structuring tool I always teach, one that students in many contexts have told me helps them in the drafting stage. The principle is very simple. Readers like to move from old information to new information; that is, they like to have the subject of a sentence contain information they have heard before and the new content to be presented in the predicate. After the new information appears in the predicate, it is old and can then appear as the subject. So the chain of information can be expressed abstractly as A + B, B + C, C + D, or old plus new, which becomes old plus new, and so on. Readers cannot process too many items of new information in a single sentence, nor do they like new before old very often; that kind of sentence has to be turned inside out to be processed. Complex material needs to be presented to readers slowly; keeping the subject the same and adding new information in successive predicates gives readers a break, as in A + B, A + C, A + D, and so on. Consider, for example, how reporter Jay Taylor introduces a complicated story about bonds by carefully controlling the rate of new information:

> The South Carolina General Assembly knows a problem when it sees one. When it saw the risks of bad barbering, it created a commission "to regulate the practice of barbering in South Carolina."
>
> The Legislature has provided for other pressing needs. It created commissions that stand guard over folk heritage, aquaculture, cosmetology, and the governor's mansion. There is even a Commission on the Distribution of Dead Human Bodies, which helps direct the research use of unidentified cadavers.
>
> But state lawmakers have never seen a problem in the less visible municipal bond industry, which funds everything from town halls and courthouses to jails and sewers. Virtually every week, a South Carolina locality issues a municipal bond to build something. Although bonds are nothing more than IOUs with interest, the transactions are complex and technical, and a wrong move can cost thousands of dollars.

The paradox of reading is that we notice we are reading only when we are having trouble—that is, when the writer has not controlled the flow of information carefully enough for us to move through the text effortlessly. In any world of writing, public or private sector, plenty of texts can be found that illustrate information out of control: too many new pieces of information per sentence, too few cues for constructing the text, new information coming before old, nominalizations, and noun-plus-noun-plus-noun constructions. Criticizing unreadable texts and offering lists of don'ts is a traditional workshop technique, and perhaps accounts for the negative image of English teachers in popular culture. But I have always believed that writers gain the most from teaching that offers positive instructions—conceptual tools for constructing texts—so that explaining *what to do* to meet readers' needs, rather than *what not to do*, is the goal of my presentations. We do know much more than we used to about what makes writing readable; writing consultants need to be popularizers of linguistic insights, not just usage police.

THE ETHOS OF AGENCY WRITING

Every public agency worries about its image. And dedicated public administrators carry visions of how they would like their agency to be perceived. They have reasoned answers to my question, "What kind of person do you want your agency to be?" Their responses always have to do with concern, commitment, honesty, ethics; they tend to see their mission as protectors, protecting the public from danger or confusion or suffering or misused resources. Such qualities can be translated easily into *qualities of style.* Agency writers need to be persuaded that such a translation works two ways: The qualities of the style of their documents will be translated as the agency's ethos. What sort of ethos do you want your documents to project? What qualities of writing will convey that image? The answers, of course, are announced structures and purposes, a controlled flow of information, changing levels of abstraction, clear explanations, sentences with agents that are not too long and sometimes very short, understandable language, visual information, concise instructions, white space, graphics that emphasize structure and purpose. Governing all of these choices must be a sure sense of audience, an awareness of what words will work. DHEC, for example, in its materials on contraception knows that for some audiences the words "rubber" and "sex" work better than "condom" and "intercourse." DHEC sometimes goes so far as to use focus groups to test choices of diction.

The final emphasis of my workshop is stylistic—because style *is* the agency—but again I try to offer do's rather than don'ts, tools rather than criticisms. Instead of focusing on bad sentences, I like to use good ones, even great ones, and ask participants to imitate them. Thus, painlessly they pick up a few schemes and tropes, among them parallel structure, anaphora, and antithesis. Their sentences, like their belts, I tell them, will get longer as they get older; they should fight both tendencies. But because they probably will write long sentences, they had best know how to control them.

A WRITING COURSE FOR PUBLIC ADMINISTRATORS

Of course, 2- or 3-hour writing workshops, as Kuehner noted, can hardly change a lifetime of writing habits. The real solution for many agency writers is surely that unit of time dear to all writing teachers, the semester-long course. I have taught such a course, "Effective Communication for Public Administrators," in the graduate program in public administration at my university—but only once. All those involved agreed on the course's relevance to such a degree; none knew how to fund it across department lines. As has been noted elsewhere in this volume, complaining about the quality of writing is a much commoner activity than investing in its improvement. Public administrators, however, are highly organized professionally and aware of their reputation for bad writing, so designing a writing course for an MPA program makes sense, though finding a supportive home for it may be problematic.

The course that I taught with my colleague Elisabeth Alford for the graduate students in the MPA program assumed that they were employed full time as public administrators. We asked our students to use their agency writing tasks to fulfill the writing assignments of the course. A number of short pieces were handed in, each accompanied by an analysis of context, as we defined it: Contexts of writing include audiences, purposes, the writer's relationship to the audience, the specific problem, and as much else as you can discover about the "environment" of the writing. Students also produced a résumé, a short report with computer-generated illustrations, a case study of a piece of agency communication, and an oral report. Meanwhile, they were keeping a writer's log detailing and analyzing all of their on-the-job writing. Their semester's goal was a writing portfolio, which included, in final form, the major assignments and was intended to be professionally useful. Our course outline explained:

> You can use it for a reference or document file, consulting it when you need to write similar pieces in the future. If you assign writing to subordinates, you can use selections from the portfolio to demonstrate important features of writing in your agency. You can also use the entire file or selections from it when preparing an application for a promotion or a new position.

We also included units on computer graphics, oral presentations, group dynamics, press releases, and collaborative writing.

The class members who were employed in public agencies made good use of our assignments. Those who were full-time students, rather than agency staffers, were less successful and somewhat suspicious of our description of agency writing tasks. The solution to funding such a course and limiting enrollment to actual agency writers requires closer collaboration between state govenment and the university—better symbiosis. Ideally, a consortium of agencies would contract with the educational institution to provide a semester-long course, free staffwriters to attend classes, and furnish writing samples and case study materials for use in the classroom. Such a collaborative venture, though charged with potential problems, would benefit English department faculty—providing them with a closer view of the writing requirements of government—as well as students.

BUILDING ON THE INTERACTION

For me, the real reason for consulting has always been to sharpen, improve, and redirect my classroom teaching. My involvement in public life, like my work in newsrooms, has made me more confident of what I know about real-world discourse. Watching and participating in the processes of government has also sharpened my sense that, in the United States, we do not do a very good job of teaching our young people how to be good citizens and how to use the literacy we have dedicated our lives to teaching them as an instrument for positive change in their communities. Thus, I have begun to search for projects that enable students to place their texts in public contexts. Recently, Columbia's newspaper, *The State*, ran a series of articles on what was wrong with our city, why its economy was stagnant, its downtown abandoned, its reputation always overshadowed by Charlotte and Charleston. I reproduced the series for my class, Rhetoric for Writers, and we talked about communities, the ones they came from, the one we were now in. Their assignment was to make some kind of a case for improving the community, to complete a project called Arguing for Columbia. At first I tried to devise community contacts for them, then I decided to let them do the work, make their own contacts, and find their own information according to their own interests.

As usual, they surprised me with their inventiveness, initiative, and "street smarts." *Lars* from New Jersey chose to get involved in the controversy over the proposed ice hockey rink for Columbia (and was appalled by the low level of the report produced by a sports consultant firm for city council). *Vicki* wanted to argue for women in business, especially African American and Caucasian women working together in the business community. What she discovered about the politics of race and gender from an African-American woman who had compiled the *Women's Yellow Pages* made the rhetorical theories we had been reading relevant in a new way. Some students, in researching what bothered them, turned into investigative reporters. *Tonya* followed her hunch and wrote an exposé of the different rules applied by local police to Black night clubs versus White ones. *Catherine*, who worked in a pool hall, knew that the video poker machines were making a lot of money that escaped state taxes. The argument she wrote for tighter licensing and new tax laws interested one of the *State's* editorial writers, who helped her polish her argument. *Sharon* was outraged by proposed legislation on sentencing guidelines for perpetrators of domestic violence; her argument went to every state legislator. Some of the students who started out to find fault found instead considerable good news and wrote positive feature stories. *Michael*, after a thorough search for flaws, argued that the county library system was a wonderful public resource, and *Michelle* told us what a great place Columbia was for raising a family, and why. In fulfilling this assignment, they all learned more about the reality of audience than I could ever have taught them had I relied only on theoretical explanations. They also learned something real about the complexities of public life, public agencies, public decision making processes, and texts in public contexts.

Sending students out beyond the confines of the classroom, after equipping them with our best rhetorical knowledge, is one way to entice them into citizenship, to show them that their texts can become public texts. The community, after all, is not out there. It is us. And we have a right and a responsibility to write it well.

ACKNOWLEDGMENTS

I would like to thank all of the state employees who took the time to explain their work to me and to provide me with their documents: Daniel O'Connor, David Williams, Mary Bostick, Jerry Dell Gimarc, Jan Tuten, David King, Karen Kuehner, Philip Grose, Jane Thesing, Jan Stucker, Alicia Leeke, and many others.

WORKS CITED

Berkenkotter, Carol. "Evolution of a Scholarly Forum: *Reader,* 1977–1988." In *A Sense of Audience in Written Communication.* Ed. Gesa Kirsch and Duane H. Roen. Newbury Park CA: Sage, 1990. 191–215.

Bogert, Judith B. W. and Rebecca B. Worley. *Managing Business Communications: An Applied Process Approach.* Englewood Cliffs NJ: Prentice Hall, 1988.

Brodkey, Linda. "Modernism and the Scene of Writing." *College English* 49 (1987): 396–418.

Closing the Gap: A Call to Action. Recommendations of the South Carolina Task Force on Minority Health, 1990.

Code of Laws of South Carolina 1976. Title 44. Vol. 15A. State of South Carolina: 1985.

1984 Cumulative Supplement: Code of Laws of South Carolina 1976. Binder 24A. State of South Carolina: 1985.

A Decade in Review and Issues for the 1990's: A Report on the Health and Environment of South Carolina. Columbia, SC: SC Department of Health and Environmental Control, 1990.

de Tocqueville, Alexis. *The Old Regime and The French Revolution.* Trans. Stuart Gilbert. Garden City NY: Doubleday, 1955.

"Drafting Rules for Uniform or Model Acts," As Approved by the Executive Committee of the National Conference of Commissioners on Uniform State Laws, July, 1983.

Drennon, Catherine. *A Consumer's Guide to Long Term Care Insurance in South Carolina.* Columbia, SC: Joint Legislative Committee on Aging, 1990.

"An Economy Adrift," *The State*, Sept. 5–10, 1993.

Finding the Falls: A Guide to Twenty-five of the Upstate's Outstanding Waterfalls. Columbia, SC: SC Wildlife and Marine Resources Department, 1990.

Foucault, Michel. "What is an Author?" *The Foucault Reader*. Ed. Paul Rabinow. New York: Pantheon, 1984. 101–120.

Hayakawa, S. I. *Language in Thought and Action.* New York: Harcourt, 1939, 1972.

Herndl, Carl G., Barbara A. Fennell, and Carolyn R. Miller. "Understanding Failures in Organizational Discourse: The Accident at Three Mile Island and the Shuttle *Challenger* Disaster." In *Textual Dynamics of the Professions: Historical and Contemporary Studies of Writing in Professional Communities*. Ed. Charles Bazerman and James Paradis. U of Wisconsin P, 1992. 279–305.

Kirsch, Gesa. "Experienced Writers' Sense of Audience and Authority: Three Case Studies." In *A Sense of Audience in Written Communication*. Ed. Gesa Kirsch and Duane H. Roen. Newbury Park CA: Sage, 1990. 216–230.

Lakoff, George. *Women, Fire, and Dangerous Things: What Categories Reveal about the Mind.* U of Chicago P, 1987.

Lesser, Charles H. *Relic of the Lost Cause: The Story of South Carolina's Ordinance of Secession.* Columbia, SC: SC Department of Archives and History, 1990.

A Management Review of the Savannah Valley Authority. South Carolina Legislative Audit Council, 1993.

Phelps, Louise Wetherbee. "Audience and Authorship: The Disappearing Boundary." In *A Sense of Audience in Written Communication*. Ed. Gesa Kirsch and Duane H. Roen. Newbury Park CA: Sage, 1990. 153–174.

Porter, James E. "Reading Presences in Texts: Audience as Discourse Community." In *Oldspeak/Newspeak: Rhetorical Transformations*. Ed. Charles W. Kneupper. Arlington, TX: Rhetoric Society of America, 1985. 241–256.

Potts, Thomas D. *Beginning a Bed and Breakfast in South Carolina: Guidelines for Development.* Columbia, SC: Cooperative Extension Service; SC Department of Parks, Recreation and Tourism, 1990.

Roth, Robert G. "Deconstructing Audience: A Post-Structuralist Rereading." *A Sense of Audience in Written Communication*. Ed. Gesa Kirsch and Duane H. Roen. Newbury Park CA: Sage, 1990. 175–187.

Small Quantity Waste Generator Manual. South Carolina Department of Health and Environmental Control, 1993.

South Carolina House of Representatives Legislative Update. Volume 11, May 1994, No. 18.

South Carolina State Register. Legislative Council of the General Assembly. State of South Carolina: 1977– .

Sperber, Dan and Deirdre Wilson. *Relevance: Communication and Cognition.* Harvard UP, 1986.

Taylor, Jay. "Money Machine Largely Unregulated," *The State*, October 16, 1994. D-1.

Women's Yellow Pages: Directory and Resource Guide. Columbia, SC, 1993–94.

CHAPTER THREE

Consulting in a Bureaucracy: Helping Government Evaluators Write Effective Reports

Joyce N. Magnotto
Old Dominion University

The situation involves an evaluator who received an unacceptable rating in the critical job dimension of writing. Although he was provided a reasonable period for improving his writing skills, he failed to do so, and he was informed that the agency intended to remove him for poor performance.

—*GAO Management News* (No. 28: 6)

In most people's minds, bureaucratic writing is synonymous with endless sentences, noun strings, acronyms, and passive voice—the hallmarks of gobbledegook. Nevertheless, many government agencies depend on written reports to achieve their missions. Bureaucrats spend much of their time writing, and, as the epigraph shows, they can be dismissed if they fail to write effectively.

For the past 8 years, I have served as a writing consultant to several federal agencies, including the Department of Labor (DOL), the General Accounting Office (GAO), and the U.S. Office of Government Ethics (OGE). The opportunity to work with federal employees presented itself to me in the serendipitous way that such challenges often do—when we least expect them! At the time, I was teaching business communications and directing a growing writing-across-the-curriculum program at a community college just east of Washington, DC. I had recently participated in the National Writing Project and had returned to graduate school to work on a doctorate in writing (after earning bachelor's and master's degrees in literature). The

69

request came from a former colleague who wanted me to teach report writing to auditors and evaluators. Somehow, the opportunity seemed to fit with the turns my career had been taking—away from teaching literature and toward my emerging expertise in teaching writing.

Since that telephone call in 1987, I have taught many writing seminars for federal agencies. I have also designed report writing courses and coached government writers in a one-on-one tutoring program. Most of my consulting has been with auditors, evaluators, and program analysts who produce financial and investigative reports on a wide range of topics.[1] These specialists work in highly charged political contexts that are always rhetorically complex. Their audiences include the U.S. Congress, other federal officials, academics, corporate managers, the public, and the media. Their overriding purpose is to effect better government—not an easy task in a world of entrenched agency policies, overly recursive review practices, and traditional methodological expectations. My role as a consultant in the unique setting of the federal bureaucracy has taught me a great deal about work-world writing.

GOVERNMENT EVALUATORS: THEIR PURPOSES, AUDIENCES, AND PRODUCTS

In 1991, GAO published 880 audit and evaluation reports, delivered 277 testimonies before congressional committees, and issued 3,906 legal decisions and opinions on topics as varied as the performance of weapon systems used in the Persian Gulf War and assessing options for improving national health care.

—(GAO Training and Education 1992–1993 Catalog 3)

Individuals who write in a bureaucracy aren't much different from writers in other institutional settings in the sense that they compose several types of documents and practice various writing processes. On a typical day, a government evaluator may scribble an informal note to a colleague assigned to the same audit team and may revise a 30-page chapter to be included in a bound, typeset report that is based on months of field work. Evaluators balance thoroughness against timeliness, accuracy against page limitations, personal autonomy against institutional mandates. They struggle to appropriate an agency "voice," to write as members of a "team," and to meet the needs of multiple audiences.

Government Evaluators. Certain federal agencies are charged by the U.S. Congress or the President with oversight and investigative responsibilities. To meet their responsibilities, the agencies hire auditors, evaluators,

---

[1] I have taught writing seminars to administrative and clerical staff, but the bulk of my work has been with evaluators, so I focus on evaluative report writing in this chapter.

examiners, and analysts (terms I will use interchangeably here). Once they are on the job, evaluators carry out their research and write reports documenting the results. Although some large agencies employ writer-editors to support the evaluators, most agencies expect the evaluators, themselves, to write up the results of their investigations.

Government auditors and evaluators are content experts who hold bachelors' degrees in specialties such as business, economics, health, accounting, and chemistry. Some have graduate degrees when they are hired; others earn graduate degrees during the course of their employment. A small number of evaluators have majored in English or have minored in technical writing; the majority have only written academic papers in the typical freshman composition sequence and in other college courses. Like the workworld writers described elsewhere in this volume, their writing expertise awaits further on-the-job development.

Report Purposes and Rhetorical Contexts. To keep Congress and the public informed on important issues, federal evaluators constantly write reports that assess ongoing programmatic activities, build cases for new government regulations, uncover fraud or ethics violations, and spur reform. The rhetorical context for investigative reports is highly complex. Sometimes, the political culture in which evaluators write competes with the "scientific" model of auditing they are required to follow. Report conclusions and recommendations are supposed to emerge from hard data. Results are expected to represent an objective reality (where unstated assumptions about truth and goodness are alive and well). To complicate matters further, the latest buzzword in government auditing is "risk management," so evaluators must strike a balance between costs and results. They know that *absolute* safety in a workplace may have to give way to *reasonably* safe conditions that let employers keep plants open and paychecks printed. "Why pay billions for zero risk?" is the political question driving more and more audits.

The balancing act that ensues from conflicting rhetorical aims can be seen, for example, in investigations of shipbuilding, an issue periodically researched at the Norfolk regional office of the U.S. General Accounting Office. Congressional representatives, who request shipbuilding studies, are usually concerned about the economic development of their home districts. The Navy, a major force in Tidewater, Virginia, is always concerned about the number of ships in the fleet as well as cost-containment. Evaluators assigned to investigate shipbuilding are striving for objectivity, in spite of the fact that shipbuilding influences the economic health of the city where they live and work. And finally, GAO's senior executives, who must approve all published reports, are charged with producing "accurate," "constructive," and "supported" messages. Rhetorical situations in federal agencies are intricate and complex.

Report Audiences. Government evaluators write for multiple audiences. The first readers are team members who are coauthoring the report and an immediate supervisor who reads for auditing savvy as well as quality of writing (at least that is what the evaluators think their products are being read for). But thereafter, the audience is an ever-expanding one that can be visualized as a series of concentric rings. The ring closest to the writer includes supervisors and reviewers in the agency that employs the evaluator. The next ring includes staff and agency heads at the agency being audited. Still farther out from the center are congressional staffs, senators, and representatives. Additional readers come from the media, academia, and other public communities.

Written Products. Just as writing an academic research paper depends on complex thinking and writing strategies, so does writing a government report. In both scenarios, a series of texts precedes the final product. In the course of an audit project, for example, evaluators will write most, if not all, of the following documents:

- decision papers
- records of contact and interview write-ups
- auditor's notes
- workpaper summaries
- memoranda
- letters
- notes to team members
- outlines
- executive summaries
- conference notes for presenting work in progress
- technical appendices
- headings and side captions
- tables, figures, and graphs

The final document can take the form of a single briefing report, letter report, or chapter report, but sometimes the project results in multiple "final" texts. For instance, a team investigating a health care topic may first draft written testimony to be read aloud before a Congressional committee. Next, the team may convert that testimony into a briefing report (a time-sensitive document that provides analyses, observations, and alternatives, but not recommendations). Eventually the team may produce a chapter report with findings, conclusions, and recommendations.

Written products are characteristically intertextual in a bureaucracy. Certain topics (the Mining Law of 1872, for example) have been unfolding for decades and require annual reviews or have built-in dates for follow-up reports. Periodically, such topics generate long reports with recommendations for Congress; in the interim, evaluators produce short reports that summarize the latest developments surrounding the issue. Timeliness, funding, human resources, and political exigencies affect choices about the products a team produces (just as they affect other report decisions).

Report Conventions. For the most part, the writing conventions at various government agencies support the missions of the agencies. For example, workpapers (the equivalent of notecards or a research log for an academic paper) are prepared according to specific format requirements that enable groups of evaluators to share data (especially important in long-term investigations). A set of workpapers can include, among other things, testimonials, cost schedules, and records of contact. Each record of contact in a set of workpapers has a prescribed heading with spaces designated for the job code, participants' names, location of the meeting, purposes for the interview, date, and a "filename," as can be seen in Fig. 3.1. The result of such conventions is a consistent means of storing data so that other evaluators can locate information and so that reports can be indexed (a process of cross-referencing every claim made in a report to specific data in the workpapers).[2]

Another set of report conventions involves production designs for the written products that agencies publish. The "blue covers" used to bind certain GAO reports signify in-depth investigations that are several chapters long with findings, conclusions, and recommendations. Shorter letter reports, on the other hand, must meet strict page limitations. For most products, type font and size, margin width, and placement of headings and side captions are all standardized. Certain features appear in the same order in every document: a letter of transmittal, an executive summary, findings chapters, conclusions, recommendations, agency comments (what the agency under investigation said in response to a draft version of the report), and technical appendices. Figure 3.2 shows the table of contents for a GAO report on welfare programs. The headers and footers, the list of abbreviations, and the type fonts follow design conventions set forth in the agency's *Communications Manual.* The use of verbs in titles for findings chapters supports the injunction to put the main message up front.

---

[2]At GAO, workpaper preparation is taught to new hires in a self-paced training course that covers purposes of workpapers, collecting and analyzing evidence, guidelines for individual workpapers, guidelines for constructing a workpaper bundle, and responsibilities for safeguarding workpapers.

Job Code—xxxxx
Record of Contact

Filename: xxxxxxxxxx   Prepared by: xxxxx xxxxxxxxxxxxxxxx
                                             Date prepared: xx/xx/xx

PURPOSE: To obtain the U.S. Marine Corps' (USMC) perspective on questions pertaining
               to funding, performance indicators, personnel, and policies/practices as they
               relate to ground and aviation unit level maintenance activities.

AGENCY PARTICIPANTS:

(SEE ATTACHED LIST OF MEETING ATTENDEES)

RESEARCH PARTICIPANTS:

_____, Assistant Director

_____, Regional Assignment Manager

_____, Evaluator

LOCATION: USMC Headquarters, 3033 Wilson Blvd, Room 728, Arlington, VA

DATE: _____

RESULTS

USMC officials provided the following information addressing the relationship between funding,
performance indicators, personnel, policies/practices, and unit level maintenance activities:

Too Early to Predict Unit Level Maintenance Funding Shortfalls

        USMC officials noted that, in fiscal year 1993, depot level reparables (DLRs) were "free
issued" to units. However, beginning in fiscal year 1994, units had to start purchasing DLRs.
Although it is expected that a funding shortfall will exist, it is too early to predict its magnitude.
The officials......

FIG. 3.1. Format used for record of contact.

WRITING AS PROCESS IN A BUREAUCRACY

*Reports took from 6 to 9 months to process from the report conference to
publication. Teams in the two divisions produced, on the average, 19 drafts.
Approximately 13 different reviewers looked at the drafts with over 46 informal
meetings taking place among different individuals. The number of comments on
a single draft ranged from 10 to over 1,000. Some reports accumulated over
4,000 comments from first to final draft.*

        (Susan Kleimann, Vertical Collaboration: The Report Review Process *6)*

Even though the ultimate success of a government report depends on teamwork, experienced evaluators spend a considerable amount of time composing drafts alone at their computer terminals. They must also plan, draft, revise, and polish their texts within a bureaucratic culture that situates teamwork inside a hierarchy. Government writers cope with this sometimes schizophrenic composing culture in different ways, but their writing processes generally can be characterized as highly recursive, collaborative, and technologically sophisticated. They become adroit at moving between individual and group composing. Talk seems to ease the transition.

Collaborative Processes. Whenever I have worked as a writing consultant for a government agency, I have been struck by how much government writers talk to one another about their audit topics *and* their writing processes. The talk signifies the extensive interaction that is necessary to bring a multifaceted project to fruition. Usually the conversation begins as soon as a request is received from Congress and a report team is formed. The team includes an evaluator in charge (EIC) and one or more staff members. Although there is variation in how teams execute their tasks and in the final products they produce, all members talk to one another not only about the audit but also about writing the report.

These "process" conversations begin with initial report conferences and continue through some or all of the following:

- storyboarding
- corresponding with requestor
- preparing workpapers
- drafting and revising
- referencing and indexing
- report review
- seeking agency comments
- design and production

Several evaluators have told me that on rare occasions involving really tight deadlines, they and their supervisors will isolate themselves (for example, at a conference center outside the city or in a hotel room near their downtown office), and will work nonstop to produce a draft. They claim that the resulting document seems to require less revision as it cycles through the policy and review offices. When questioned further, evaluators state that this intensive process produces more coherent reports because it forces extended face-to-face talk among professionals from different levels of the bureaucratic hierarchy. The report is talked through, worked through, and written through simultaneously. A downside, however, is the heightened pressure for accountability. One evaluator felt like he was on the witness stand during these

Welfare Programs: Ineffective Federal Oversight Permits Costly Automated System Problems

(Fig. 3.2. continues)

Abbreviations

AFDC	Aid to Families with Dependent Children
GAO	General Accounting Office
HHS	Health and Human Services
IMTEC	Information Management and Technology Division
USDA	U.S. Department of Agriculture

FIG. 3.2. Table of contents for GAO report on welfare programs.

marathon sessions. He was decidedly uncomfortable about the interrogation he received from an associate director but was convinced that the team produced a good report because of the process. Admittedly, this particular example is an extreme version of the ordinary report scenario; nevertheless, it highlights the talk–write cycles that characterize collaboration.

Recursiveness. As Susan Kleimann's comment at the beginning of this section indicates, recursiveness is built into hierarchical structures, and so it is not surprising that government writing processes are highly recursive. A document is drafted, sent to a supervisor, commented on, sent back to the team, sent through the supervisor again, sent on to the next level of supervision, commented on, returned to the team, and so forth. Kleimann's research at GAO led her to develop "complexity charts" of the multiple stops that each report makes before it is published ("Complexity of Workplace Review" 525). The chart in Fig. 3.3 captures the "ping pong" effect of report review when evaluators send a document forward, and reviewers bounce it back to the team. On the positive side, review becomes a type of "vertical collaboration" in which more experienced evaluators mentor less experienced evaluators through helpful review comments (Kleimann, "Reciprocal Relationship" 56). The rounds of drafting (along with the planned intertextuality of written products) allow for exploratory drafts and for reports that function as pieces of bigger pictures rather than as definitive pronouncements. (The problems that recursive review causes are discussed in more detail later.)

Technological Sophistication. Technology is an important aspect of government writing. At the agencies where I consult, evaluators have personal computers and access to Internet and E-mail, and they have had such access since the 1980s. These days, they carry laptop or notebook computers to audit sites. As their reports progress, project teams hold teleconferences with fellow auditors located at regional sites across the country. Evaluators are not put off by technology, and they readily offer me advice when I use computers in training situations. It is also becoming more common for government agencies to deliver writing courses via two-way interactive television. In many respects, government agencies are creating virtual spaces for writing. (See Moran 1992 for a discussion of academic and worksite applications of virtual writing spaces.)

WRITING TRAINING FOR EVALUATORS

GAO's goal for reducing rework is to cut in half over the next 3 years the number of days from the first draft of a product to its issuance, with a ten percent reduction in the first year.

—*GAO Management News* (No. 29: 1)

Government agencies help evaluators with their writing by assigning writer-editors to report teams and by arranging one-to-one mentoring through-

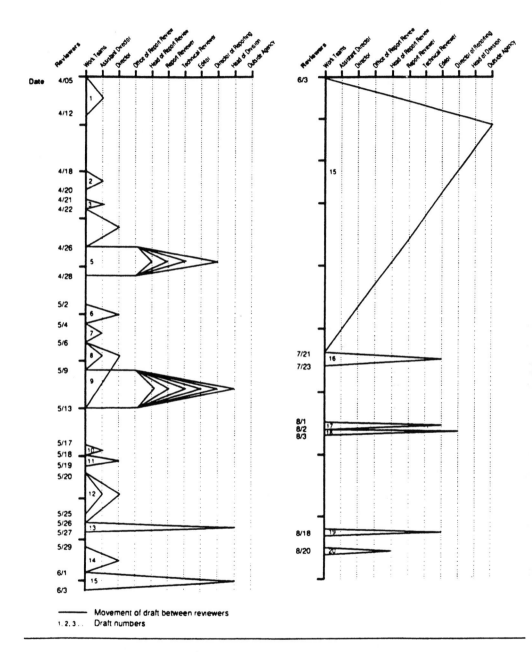

FIG. 3.3. Ping-pong effect of report review. From Kleimann (1991). Reprinted with permission of *Technical Communication*, published by the Society for Technical Communication, Arlington, VA.

out the review process. Some agencies provide formal writing training as well.

Training Institute at GAO. The U.S. General Accounting Office has its own Training Institute (TI), and within that institute is a group responsible for writing training. In addition to its full-time employees, the group hires consultants to deliver courses it develops both in- and out-of-house. Most writing courses are designed in collaboration with evaluators and others who are target audiences for the courses. TI produces a 140-page catalog explaining training requirements and listing courses. Eleven courses are dedicated to writing; several other courses have major writing components. Writing courses are available to both professional and support staff.

Many GAO writing consultants are academics who have earned excellent teaching evaluations. All have written extensively themselves. The Training Institute further prepares writing consultants in several ways: (a) having them observe courses before they teach them, (b) providing instructor manuals for each course, (c) pairing 'new' consultants with seasoned ones in team-taught courses, (d) holding annual meetings of writing consultants, (e) providing access to many GAO documents, (f) providing a consultant's handbook. TI also recruits experienced evaluators to do two-year stints as trainers, and pairs these evaluator/trainers with outside writing consultants in such courses as Executive Summary Writing, Report Review, and Report Writing and Message Development.

Writing Training at OGE. The U.S. Office of Government Ethics (OGE) is a small agency that finds it more efficient to hire outside writing consultants than to maintain full-time writing instructors on staff. Rather than developing courses from scratch, OGE borrows writing courses from GAO, modifying the courses slightly to fit their needs, or asks outside consultants to bring in generic courses. For example, new examiners are given a 2-day course within their first 2 years at OGE. The course combines elements from intermediate and more advanced GAO courses. An associate director arranges the consultant's visit. Follow-up support is ad hoc. Tight budgets usually mean writing training gets postponed.

Writing Training at DOL. The Department of Labor (DOL) is a huge agency that approaches writing training differently than either GAO or OGE does. One way DOL provides training is through a 2-week retreat held every other year for auditors and evaluators. Those attending the retreat can elect a 3-day writing component, which is a compilation of courses borrowed from GAO and adapted by consultants to the needs of DOL auditors. I find it interesting that DOL auditors frequently describe the writing they do on the job as formulaic and filled with boilerplate. Nonetheless, they express the same frustration that GAO and OGE employees express: Supervisors seem to make arbitrary changes to their reports. Writing consultants must, of course, take an agency's culture into account when designing training for that agency.

The Writing Curriculum. In many ways, GAO represents an ideal approach to writing training in government. The curriculum is coherent, extensive, and constantly being revised to meet agency needs. Courses are tailored for staff, evaluators, managers, and senior executives (SESers). There are required courses, core courses, and electives, which are carefully sequenced. Prerequisites are listed in a catalog. Periodically, a well-informed group of writing experts makes revisions to writing courses based on evaluations that participants complete at the end of every class. Kathy Karlson, the coordinator of the writing curriculum and a full-time GAO employee, is responsible for much of the success of the GAO program. She is knowledgeable about current writing research, attends professional meetings such as the Conference on College Composition and Communication, presents conference papers, and publishes articles on government writing.

Despite the informed approaches to writing training at GAO, other federal agencies seem stymied by the very conflict troubling academia: Are writing classes a service (one that English departments provide for universities), or is writing a distinct field of study? GAO addresses the issue by opting for "hybrid" courses that develop staff both as writers and as content experts. For example, Executive Summary Workshop, a course developed by evaluators and writing experts working collaboratively, combines data analysis with discourse analysis, thus helping participants use structure to support the message of the report. A sample course outline for Executive Summary Workshop can be found in Fig. 3.4.[3] Note the emphasis on logical links and readability in several modules. Participants are taught sophisticated revision strategies such as marking continuous and discontinuous logical connections.

Making Course Arrangements. Writing consultants benefit from the priority government agencies give to professional development and on-the-job training. Agencies have training systems in place and training officers to take care of scheduling courses, booking rooms, coordinating registration, and providing materials.[4] As a government consultant, I always find myself assigned to user-friendly classrooms with comfortable tables and chairs. Flip charts and white boards replace chalkboards; audio–visual equipment is readily available. Enrollments are limited to a number that would make high

---

[3]Figures 3.4 through 3.9 are taken from GAO training manuals and are reprinted courtesy of the U.S. General Accounting Office.

[4]In small government agencies without training officers, a manager usually arranges courses for her or his staff on an as-needed basis. For the writing consultant, the manager or training officer is a valuable link who can clarify the objectives of the training and describe the participants' goals. This person also knows the history of the agency and the success of prior training programs.

Course Outline for Executive Summary Workshop

Module 1:	Introduction
Module 2:	The Executive Summary: Communicating the Report Message
Module 3:	Readability: Understanding the Concept
Module 4:	The Critical Link: The Logical Flow Through the Sections
Module 5:	The RIB and the Principal Findings: Raising and Answering Questions
Module 6:	Other Sections of the Executive Summary
Module 7:	Revising for Readability: Logic Markers
Module 8:	Revising for Readability Attitude Markers
Module 9:	The Relationship of the Executive Summary to the Final Report
Module 10:	Summary and Evaluation
Appendix 1	Writer-Based and Reader-Based Writing
Appendix 2	Product Review Checklist

FIG. 3.4. Course outline for ESW.

school and university teachers envious. Often two instructors co-teach a course of 20 or fewer participants. In such an ideal environment, intensive, personal instruction and small group work are the norm.

Selecting Course Materials. Government training materials are in the public domain, and writing consultants can—if they choose—adapt these materials instead of inventing them. At the General Accounting Office, detailed course manuals, designed by writing consultants, evaluators, and training experts, incorporate composition theory and adult learning theory. Their bibliographies contain names that composition instructors would easily recognize—Joseph Williams, William Zinsser, Richard Lanham, and Linda Flower, to name a few. The list of assumptions in Fig. 3.5 comes from the instructor's manual for Writing Seminar, a one-day workshop featuring in-depth peer review of writing samples that participants bring to the session. Figure 3.6 reproduces the course objectives for the same workshop. Note the positive tone, the emphasis on collaboration, and the integration of writing and reading processes.

Writing Seminar Assumptions

Writing Seminar is grounded on several assumptions, many of which may be familiar to you. These assumptions come from composition and adult learning theory as well as training experience at GAO.

- In a supportive, nonthreatening atmosphere, a writer can practice separating his or her ego from a document. A writer can learn that comments about a document are not comments about the person who wrote it.

- Thoughtful, candid readers can help a writer see what *is* on the page, not what the writer *hopes* is on the page.

- All writers at times feel that they have nothing to say and what they have said is said badly. Talking about writing provides writers with crucial social support.

- Readers can help a writer *resee* a document.

- Collaborative writing and revision can be improved by (1) developing a vocabulary about writing and (2) applying specific writing principles.

- There is a significant difference between knowing that a document has a problem and knowing how to define the specific problem(s). A structured reading process helps readers and writers diagnose and remedy weakness(es) in a document.

- A writer revises more effectively when he or she looks at a document globally, considering the audience's needs, instead of looking for errors in a sentence-by-sentence approach.

- A writer needs to *test* his or her document against an updated understanding of the purpose, audience, and subject.

FIG. 3.5. Assumptions on which *Writing Seminar* is based.

In the Writing Seminar course, each participant's draft is read and analyzed by other participants in a day-long response group. The class is limited to six participants, and the analysis is guided by sets of questions on six topics: background, content, structure and organization, paragraphs, sentences, and overall effect. Figure 3.7 shows a list of questions and a worksheet for content analysis. The course stresses rhetorical context as a frame for making writing decisions.

Figure 3.8 reproduces the course outline for POWER, a two-day workshop on report writing and review. The modules move sequentially from structuring a whole report to structuring individual sections to using headings and tables of contents as reader cues. Paragraph and sentence issues are treated in the rhetorical context of the report. The modules replicate the

Introduction to Writing Seminar

Overview	Writing Seminar provides an opportunity to assess and improve professional writing skills. You will read and respond to writing samples in order to strengthen your planning, writing, and revising skills as well as collaborative writing skills.

Course Objectives	As a *writer*, you will develop skills in

- articulating the purpose, audience, subject, and writer's role for writing tasks;

- increasing readability of your writing;

- listening openly and responding appropriately to a discussion of your writing;

- evaluating the clarity of your writing;

- assessing the organization of your work;

- checking paragraphs for unity and coherence; and

- eliminating sentence problems such as inappropriate voice, prepositional overuse, and wordiness.

As a *reader*, you will develop skills in

- increasing awareness of all of the above and

- responding constructively and specifically to others' writing.

FIG. 3.6. Course objectives for *Writing Seminar.*

order of concerns on the "Checklist for Writers and Reviewers" that appears in GAO's *Writing Guidelines* (see Fig. 3.9).

WRITING PROBLEMS IN GOVERNMENT AGENCIES

By the twenty-fifth draft, they finally liked it, and by that time it was amazingly similar to what I had written originally. It had gone full circle.
—(Government evaluator participating in a writing seminar)

Audit reports are rhetorically complex. They must serve multiple audiences (both hostile and friendly, expert and nonexpert) and must meet multiple purposes (those of the writers, the requestors, and the agencies). Their subject matter is usually technical, but their recommendations will be acted upon by generalists (congressmen and women, agency officials). Not only must report writers negotiate these rhetorical exigencies; they must also construct a role for themselves in keeping with the agency's "voice" or persona. Such sophisticated rhetorical situations preclude one-draft, produced-on-demand documents; such situations require a great deal of thinking and writing time.

Federal budget cuts and hiring freezes compound writing problems at government agencies. Program analyses and audits can save taxpayers money but, first, money must be spent to hire and train expert evaluators. In the 1990s, fewer staff members are available to respond to a growing number of requests for audits. The resulting production delay causes such frustration for public servants (not to mention their customers) that federal agencies are continuously working to address the issue. Several factors related to timeliness surface whenever I consult with evaluators; lengthy report review and inefficient writing practices of new hires are chief among them.

Lengthy Report Review. Report review is a critical step in government report writing. Managers at each level of the hierarchy read the document and analyze it from their specialized perspectives (legal, technical, methodological, political). Such procedures assure credibility and accuracy, but this built-in recursiveness is, in fact, both positive and negative. Evaluators become frustrated with the time the review takes, and they perceive review comments to be more arbitrary than substantive. Their response may be to send drafts forward too soon, and thus a vicious circle can begin. The unpolished draft is returned with numerous review comments and must be thoroughly revised. A related problem grows out of the virtual writing culture that agencies are nurturing. Evaluators tell of supervisors who, in attempts to meet deadlines, appropriate disks from staff and revise texts electronically. Traces of "whose work was whose" are erased, and, more importantly, the team's prerogative to have a say about substantive changes is compromised.

Writing Practices of New Hires. When individuals are hired as government auditors or evaluators, the writing practices they bring to the workplace are those they developed during undergraduate and graduate school. As students they were rewarded for displaying "received" knowledge and for following the conventions of a particular discipline. In some instances, they were praised for a sophisticated personal style, but they were rarely treated as developing writers.[5] They were students whose goal was to finish being students. Collaboration was generally discouraged (and sometimes considered cheating). Furthermore, their college writing had a very short shelf life, and 98 percent of it had an audience of one professor.

---

[5]See Lester Faigley's *Fragments of Rationality* for a thorough discussion of modern and postmodern constructions of students. See also my study of how students are constructed as "non-writers" in school contexts (Magnotto 156-57).

Topic 2: Content Analysis

Overall Precision	1.	Is the writer's meaning clear? Does the sample have any vague terms or phrases that could force a reader to guess among a range of possible meanings? Are terms used consistently?
	2.	Does the focus of the sample change unexpectedly?
	3.	Does the content fulfill the sample's purpose?
	4.	Is the sample complete? Does it answer all of a reader's possible questions? Does it counter probable objections?
Message		Massive amounts of information are gathered for any GAO assignment. However, merely to report the information is insufficient. Writers need to communicate their understanding of the facts by forming clear, specific message statements and by selecting and ordering information in support of these statements. Facts do not "speak" for themselves.
		To help you visualize the structure of the writing sample, complete the worksheet on page 9. After you have completed the worksheet (filled in the boxes), answer the following questions:
	a.	Is the message (thesis) clearly stated?
	b.	Is the message adequately supported?
	c.	Is each support sufficiently developed with details and examples?
	d.	Does the sample contain details or examples that are not directly related to a support?

FIG. 3.7a. Questions for content analysis.

In other words, expertise in college writing does not assure an easy transition to expertise in workplace writing. In fact, one may impede the other. Novice evaluators find that government agencies want reports structured deductively rather than inductively or narratively. They also find that government agencies require collaboration, expect boilerplate and repetition to be used for efficiency, and demand final products that speak with an agency "voice." Individual style is unacceptable. The document must be "useful, timely, accurate, complete, constructive, convincing, objective, clear and simple, and concise," to quote the GAO *Communications Manual* (1989, 12.1-4 to 12.1-6). The audience will be diverse and large; the shelf life of the product may be decades long.

Needless to say, then, new evaluators must reconstruct their individual writing practices to meet the agency's requirements. First, they must learn to

Deductive Structure Worksheet

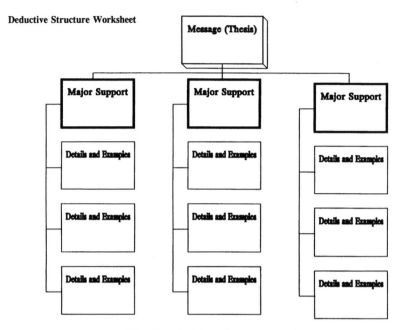

FIG. 3.7b. Worksheet for content analysis.

balance auditing and writing to meet deadlines, which are the rule rather than the exception in the workplace. In bureaucracies, individual deadlines are embedded in project deadlines, agency deadlines, and political deadlines. Too often, new evaluators postpone writing because they believe that writing is merely the transcription of thought and that thinking precedes (and is independent of) writing. They seldom perceive writing itself as a means of analysis. Second (but related to the first issue), new auditors are prone to retell the history of the audit. They focus on what they have done rather than on what it means. The result is a narrative structure that does not meet the needs of busy readers who expect to find the bottom line and the "so what?" up-front. Third, new evaluators may have an acceptable command of standard edited English, but they seldom have much skill in manipulating grammar and usage to support a report's message. As students, they learned grammar and usage rules by practicing with discrete sentences in workbook exercises. They now need to master the rhetorical implications of sentence structure and diction. Finally, new evaluators have little experience with incorporating written and oral response from multiple reviewers. They become defensive about review comments because they may not know how to revise their drafts in response to those comments.

As Jamie MacKinnon discovered in his study of college graduates making the transition from school writing to organizational writing, "the writing-related changes were considerable, consequential, and a shock for some

Course Outline for Power

Introduction	Report Writing
Module 1:	**Deductive Structure States the Main Point First**
	Deductive structure allows the reader to understand the writer's main point easily and rapidly. The writer moves from the global to the specific.
Module 2:	**Chapters and Sections Build on Deductive Structure**
	Chapters and sections written with deductive structure become more unified and coherent thereby improving readability and making the material more accessible.
Module 3:	**The Table of Contents Outlines the Report**
	The Table of Contents conveys the structure of the report's message and the logical relationships between main ideas.
Module 4:	**Paragraphs Emphasize Deductive Structure**
	Deductive structure within paragraphs depends on topic sentences to present the main idea. Unity results from supporting sentences.
Module 5:	**Coherence Depends on Order**
	Coherence depends on order, repetition, parallelism, and transitions to strengthen paragraph effectiveness.
Module 6:	**Strong Sentences Depend on Good Structure**
	Effective sentences result from good structure based on proper word order, voice, and citation; strong verbs; and limited use of prepositions.
Module 7:	**Effective Reviewing Improves the Report and Trains the Writer**
	Supervisors use good writing principles to improve and review products for themselves and their staff. They recognize the importance of moving from global concerns, such as the overall message and structure, to specific concerns, such as grammar and punctuation.

FIG. 3.8. Course outline for power.

participants" (50). It takes time for evaluators (or anyone else for that matter) to write successfully in a new culture. Writing consultants can play a key role in helping evaluators with the transition.

THE WRITING CONSULTANT'S ROLE
IN A BUREAUCRACY

"[H]ow we do things around here" is neither an objective given, nor merely a set of shifting conventions, but a social dynamic that has practical power for solving shared problems.

—(Thomas Miller, 70)

Checklist for Writers and Reviewers

Section/Chapter/Report Organization	Unity
—Does the report begin with an Executive Summary and Table of Contents that provide an overview of the whole report?	____
—Do the following chapters support and develop that overview?	____
—Does each chapter have a deductive paragraph that summarizes its findings?	____
—Does each chapter section begin with a paragraph that summarizes its main idea?	____
—Do advance organizers (chapters and section headings) inform the reader?	____
	Coherence
—Are the paragraphs arranged in logical order?	____
—Is repetition used to enhance coherence?	____
—Are transitions used to show how a paragraph relates to those preceding it?	____
Paragraph Organization	Unity
—Does each deductive paragraph have a precise topic sentence?	____
—Does the controlling idea of the topic sentence prepare the reader for the rest of the paragraph?	____
—Do the other sentences in the paragraph support or develop the topic sentence?	____
	Coherence
—Are the ideas arranged logically?	____
—When necessary, are sentences linked by proper use of transitions, repetition, and parallel structure?	____
Sentence Structure	Coherence
—Are all sentences concise and clearly focused?	____
—Does the structure emphasize the most important information in the sentence core?	____
—Do sentence weaknesses appear frequently?	____
Passive voice	____
Prepositional overuse	____
Nonparallel construction	____
Nominalization	____
Citation overuse	____
Weak coordination and subordination	____
Too much or inappropriate repetition	____

FIG. 3.9. Checklist from GAO's *Writing Guidelines.*

Teaching writing in workplace settings and teaching writing in the university, in my experience, are a perfect match. Knowing that each culture values writing, albeit in different ways, enables me to mediate the transition that students will make into the workplace. Additionally, as more and more employees engage in "lifelong learning" by returning to graduate school while remaining employed, I am able to mediate that "reverse" transition as well. For me, success as a teacher and consultant depends on situating writing "in the world," on constructing writing as social *praxis.*

Situating the Course.   Evaluators want to succeed in the culture where
they are employed; they want to know how their individual attempts relate
to that culture; and, as federal employees, they want to meet public needs.
Thomas Miller's explanation of "practical wisdom" (defined in his comment
at the beginning of this section), serves nicely as a foundation for a
government writing course. Once evaluators understand the full rhetorical
context of their report drafts, they are prepared to manipulate style and
structure to achieve their purposes. Writing instruction becomes situated
within the world of public service.

Responding to Participants' Texts.   The most popular segments of
courses I have presented to federal employees are those that provide direct
discussion of the participants' texts. Courses that include time for one-on-one
conferences rate highly, as do courses that use participants' writing samples
to teach rhetorical principles. Case studies that simulate an agency's composing culture (for example, cases that require coping with tight deadlines
or managing large amounts of data) work well especially when they require
participants to reflect on how they handle auditing and writing within the
constraints of a bureaucracy.

Auditors and evaluators welcome constructive criticism of their writing.
As a matter of fact, they are often quite perceptive about aspects of their
writing that need attention, and are eager to work on those issues. I always
begin conferences by asking the writer to describe the rhetorical context of
the text. Then I state my responses according to either Roger Garrison's
hierarchy (focus, content, organization, sentences, diction), Reigstad and
McAndrew's Higher and Lower Order Concerns, or the *GAO Checklist for
Writers and Reviewers* previously mentioned. I encourage participants to
consider my advice as they would that of any other expert and to seek
responses from a variety of readers. Participants value a class atmosphere
where knowledge and authority are shared.[6] Most adults are not interested
in wasting time or jockeying for grades. I, of course, welcome these attitudes
and explicitly acknowledge the professionalism of the participants.

The Language of Writing.   A writing "vocabulary" can demystify writing for accountants, auditors, and program examiners who often lack a
shared language with which to talk about writing. They appreciate clear
explanations of writing concepts and consistent use of writing terms across
courses. For example, when I define "the writing situation" as a social context
created by audience, purpose, writer's role, and subject matter, auditors
build a frame of reference that they can use when they sift through large

[6]The depth and breadth of expertise that participants bring to the seminars is impressive.
I expect to learn as well as teach, and I always do.

data dumps, trying to determine "the bottom line." By explaining Reigstad and McAndrew's Higher Order Concerns and Lower Order Concerns, I provide a schematic that helps auditors allocate their revision time. By treating writing as a "knowable" subject, I hope to encourage positive attitudes as alternatives to the negative ones evaluators may have absorbed at school.

Motivation. Auditors and program analysts do not need outside motivation. They understand after just a few months at an agency that writing is an integral part of their success. Future job assignments and promotions are based on performance appraisals that define and assess writing ability:

> Preparing and reviewing a variety of written products including issue area and assignment plans, interview write-ups, workpapers, workpaper summaries, report segments, chapters, technical appendixes, complete report or testimony, data collection instruments, internal and external correspondence, administrative documents of all types, including performance appraisals, and speeches and professional articles. (U.S. GAO, *Performance Appraisal System* 46)

The performance standard for a "fully successful" rating in written communication includes the following as *one* of the criteria:

> Prepares written products that are complete, accurate, logical, and timely; uses sufficient examples to support conclusions and recommendations; prepares products that contribute to or can be incorporated into final products with some revision and that conform to GAO policy guidance. Uses complete sentences and correct grammar and spelling. (U.S. GAO, *Performance Appraisal System* 46)

It is no wonder that evaluators talk with admiration about colleagues who are great editors, or great at setting the tone for a report that is headed to a hostile audience, or great at meeting report deadlines. Writing consultants can tap into this motivation by prefacing lessons with reminders of the practical value of writing training.

Assumptions. Bureaucrats and compositionists alike could benefit from laying their assumptions about writing out on the table and examining them. Evaluators respect a consultant who states the assumptions behind the course she is presenting. They also appreciate the opportunity to consider the assumptions they personally carry into the course. Consequently, I plan time at the beginning of a class for participants to introduce themselves, to talk about their current writing tasks, and to reflect on their beliefs about writing—whether those beliefs remain unchanged from freshman composition or have matured in the workplace.

New evaluators especially appreciate open and frank discussion of how to make the transition to workplace writing. Because of their experiences with school writing, they may see reviewers' comments as arbitrary or think that a supervisor changed the draft to justify her or his job. Sometimes new evaluators admit that they try to "psych out" a supervisor, just as they psyched out college teachers who assigned a paper. (Unfortunately, if the evaluator sends forward a very rough draft and a supervisor rewrites it, the new evaluator's assumptions are confirmed.) In government writing courses, time spent discussing authorship and authority in different discourse communities is time well spent.

Vertical Collaboration. In her groundbreaking work on the role of "review" in government report writing, Susan Kleimann describes several models the process may follow. The most successful type of review is an overlay of "contributing expertise" that allows "all types of expertise [to] become necessary and valued" ("Reciprocal" 70). In contrast to the expert–novice dichotomies that theorists tell us are out of step with postmodernism, vertical collaboration is a reciprocal activity that enhances the written product. As a writing consultant, I have found that discussing "review" as "vertical collaboration" makes sense to evaluators and allays some of their frustrations with bureaucratic roadblocks. The discussion can be augmented with a live or videotaped interview with a reviewer who describes the broader context of the agency's mission. Evaluators are eager to know what reviewers are looking for and need reassurance that reviewers make choices based on their knowledge of how government works over the long term. Perhaps the reviewer asks that a report's recommendations be softened because the agency under review has already implemented some changes in its practices. Perhaps a reviewer deletes a section from a report because he or she has just learned of a new Congressional request for a far-reaching audit of multiple agencies.

Seamlessness. Experienced evaluators see writing as so enmeshed with audit work that the distinction between "doing" research and "writing up" research is quite blurred. This is a notable departure from the separation of *writing* courses from *content* courses that remains prevalent in academic contexts. Paradoxically, the writing consultant may find it necessary to "tease out" writing issues from auditing issues in order to teach rhetorical strategies. By explicitly discussing writing and auditing as distinct activities, consultants and evaluators can analyze how they are interrelated. Such discussion helps evaluators become aware of the balancing act that bureaucratic writing re- quires, and helps them realize the extent and limitations of their roles as agents in a bureaucracy.

CONCLUSION

[T]he business writing class can provide a forum for bringing together—rather than dividing—the academic and professional worlds. If this is to happen, however, the emphasis must be on the broader concerns that both communities share, not on the mechanical aspects of writing a particular type of document that students will have to relearn on the job anyway.

—(Janette Lewis 89)

As I began drafting the conclusion to my portion of this book, I was rereading Susan Miller's *Textual Carnivals*. And, in that context, my musings went something like this:

What is the relationship between producing reports that affect government policy and getting a job promotion in a federal agency? What does an individual's mastery of standard edited English have to do with it? Do the people with the power to promote serve as surrogate English professors who gatekeep? Do the people with the power to promote know edited American English themselves? Do they care? AHA!!! Are writing consultants merely English teachers, in disguise, who are hired by those in power to put the stamp of approval on employees? Government agencies won't ask employees to take manners courses, but they will ask them to take writing courses until their prose meets certain standards of correctness.

Obviously, I was having a bad day. My musings seem pessimistic and reductive, but the issues they raise cannot be easily dismissed, even if they say as much about the state of writing in the academy as they do about the state of writing in the workplace. "Author"ity is always political. Government report writers are well-educated, sincere individuals who enter public service hoping their work can change the world for the better. They want to write clearly and concisely; they don't want to sound like bureaucrats. But, as theory reminds us, tradition is hegemonic, and patriarchies reproduce themselves. The cultural milieu of the federal government cannot be ignored when one works as a writing consultant within that milieu.

To put a more optimistic face on being a writing consultant, I would claim that I teach evaluators how to use structure to support meaning to achieve results that are significant. A government report can persuade Congress to spend money on childhood immunization programs, or it can spur legislation that reduces air pollution, or it can assess immigrant education to determine whether federal funding has kept pace with student increases (all topics of recent investigations). Evaluators want their readers to accept a report's recommendations and to act on those recommendations. Good writing instruction opens up numerous possibilities for conveying convincing arguments on important issues.

Let me move away from the positive and negative aspects of bureaucratic culture, though, and close with some final observations about government report writing and "school" writing:

1. The purposes of a writing task are both more explicit and more expansive for a government evaluator than they are for a student. Audit team members talk about what they hope to accomplish with a particular report and how their goals are situated in an ongoing project to get agencies to be more fiscally responsible, or to reduce waste, or to better serve their customers. Of course there are also purposes and consequences for school writing, but too often the academy defines writing as a test. Why else do so many assignments continue to be one-draft commands for a student to tell a professor what that professor already knows?[7]

2. The distinction between professionals who write and career writers (Couture and Rymer 5) is not as salient for the government evaluators I have worked with as it may be for other professionals. Auditing is power at GAO, but so is writing. Writing knowledge is not artificially separated from other critical knowledge areas (for example, technical knowledge as discussed by Don Samson elsewhere in this volume). In fact, during the act of evaluative report writing, technical knowledge and writing knowledge are inseparable. Too many school assignments ignore the "intersections" of critical knowledge areas.

3. No matter what their level of expertise, evaluators benefit from writing support, and the government agencies for whom I have consulted provide that support in many ways: in elaborate on-the-job training, in well-equipped resource centers with software such as Grammatik, in technology, and in mentoring. School writing programs have made gains in supporting writers through writing centers and computer labs, but providing the support too often remains the responsibility of the English department, rather than of the school as a whole. And as Carolyn Hill has shown, writing instruction is further marginalized by its positioning within the English department.

4. Document cycling serves two very important purposes for evaluators. It increases the likelihood of better products and it provides a working system of audience feedback. Government documents are recycled not only during review, but also into other documents over time. Rarely do students get to develop their papers over time and through various manifestations. Some government agencies do too much cycling (the 7-year time frame for

---

[7]Through my work with writing across the curriculum, I know that individual teachers assign exploratory writing and writing to learn. Still, my research shows that what counts in the academy is writing that displays received knowledge in return for a grade.

issuing regulations at one agency, for example); academia, on the other hand, does not do enough.[8]

Bureaucracies resist change, but they also sponsor change through written reports. Nowadays, more federal agencies are paying attention to the outcomes of their investigations. They are assessing which of their recommendations are enacted and are taking steps to increase accountability. In other words, agencies are following up their reports with action; they are reconceiving *writing* as a social practice. Along the same lines, the most informed agencies are rethinking the role of the writer in such a context. Evaluators are *also* writers whose aim is to compose reports that result in better government. Writing is no longer defined merely as a discrete skill to be learned once and for all; it is treated as an expertise to be developed throughout an evaluator's career. As a writing consultant, teacher, and writer myself, I find it a privilege to be involved with others who imagine writing this way.

ACKNOWLEDGMENT

Kathy Karlson, coordinator of the writing curriculum at GAO, has been instrumental in my development as a writing consultant. She also provided a thoughtful reading of a draft of this chapter.

WORKS CITED

Couture, Barbara and Jone Rymer. "Situational Exigence: Composing Processes on the Job by Writer's Role and Task Value." Spilka 4–20.

Faigley, Lester. *Fragments of Rationality: Postmodernity and the Subject of Composition.* Pittsburgh, PA: U of Pittsburgh P, 1992.

Garrison, Roger. *How a Writer Works.* Rev. ed. New York: Harper and Row, 1985.

Hill, Carolyn E. *Writing from the Margins: Power and Pedagogy for Teachers of Composition.* New York: Oxford UP, 1990.

Kleimann, Susan D. "The Complexity of Workplace Review." *Technical Communication.* Fourth Quarter (1991): 520–526.

———. "The Reciprocal Relationship of Workplace Culture and Review." Spilka 56–70.

———. "Vertical Collaboration and the Report Review Process at the U.S. General Accounting Office." Diss. U. of Maryland, 1989.

———. *Vertical Collaboration: The Report Review Process at the United States General Accounting Office.* Research summary, n.d.

Lewis, Janette S. "Adaptation: Business Writing as Catalyst in a Liberal Arts Curriculum." *Worlds of Writing: Teaching and Learning in Discourse Communities of Work,* ed. Carolyn B. Matalene. New York: Random House, 1989. 83–92.

MacKinnon, Jamie. "Becoming a Rhetor: Developing Writing Ability in a Mature, Writing-Intensive Organization." Spilka 41–55.

---

[8]For an insightful ethnography of workplace review practices see Kleimann, "Vertical Collaboration and the Report Process."

Magnotto, Joyce N. "The Construction of College Writing in a Cross-disciplinary, Community College Writing Center: An Analysis of Student, Tutor, and Faculty Representations." Diss. U. of Pennsylvania, 1991.

Miller, Susan. *Textual Carnivals: The Politics of Composition*. Carbondale: Southern Illinois UP, 1991.

Miller, Thomas P. "Treating Professional Writing as Social Praxis." *Journal of Advanced Composition* 11 (1991): 57–72.

Moran, Charles. "Computers and the Writing Classroom: A Look to the Future." *Re-Imagining Computers and Composition: Teaching and Research in the Virtual Age*, ed. Gail E. Hawisher and Paul LeBlanc. Portsmouth, NH: Boynton/Cook Heinemann, 1992. 7–23.

Reigstad, Thomas J. and Donald A. McAndrew. *Training Tutors for Writing Conferences*. Urbana, IL: NCTE and ERIC, 1984.

Spilka, Rachel, ed. *Writing in the Workplace: New Research Prospectives*. Carbondale: Southern Illinois UP, 1993.

U.S. General Accounting Office. *Communications Manual*. Office of Policy. May 1989.

———. *Management News*. Vol. 21, No. 28, April 18, 1994.

———. *Management News*. Vol. 21, No. 29, April 25, 1994.

———. *Performance Appraisal System for Band I, II, and III Employees*.

———. *Training and Education 1992–93 Catalog*. Training Institute. GAO/TI/92-1.

CHAPTER FOUR

Writing in High-Tech Firms

Don Samson
Radford University

According to the U.S. Office of Technology Assessment, *high-tech firms* are characterized by "technological innovation, the process by which society generates and uses new products and manufacturing processes" (p. 17). This definition may seem broad, but it is actually limited. Many high-tech industries (such as education) are not aiming to create new products or develop manufacturing processes. However, their work does involve technology—the application of principles of science, usually for commercial purposes. A high-tech firm, then, is one that uses advanced technology to provide goods or services in its field. The more high-tech the work a firm does, the more education or training is required to do it.

This chapter examines problems that writers encounter in high-tech firms, suggests solutions, and presents implications for teaching professional and technical writing, based on my experience as a writer in high-tech firms.

At Martin Marietta Electronics and Missile Systems, a major aerospace firm in Orlando, Florida, I began work as a consultant for the summer. I helped write and edit one of the four volumes of the successful proposal to manage Department of Energy facilities in Oak Ridge, Tennessee, and in Paducah, Kentucky. I was then hired as a senior writer/editor. For nearly 2 years, I edited short proposals (up to 100 pages), longer proposal volumes (up to 300 pages), reports and manuals, and briefing materials, primarily for Department of Defense contracts. I scheduled and supervised Presentations Department work on my projects—typing and typesetting, art production, layout, as well as printing and binding.

Many years earlier, I had worked as a technical writer at the Crouse-Hinds Company in Syracuse, New York. I wrote operation sheets for casting, machining, and assembling outdoor lighting and traffic signal equipment, and maintained a reference file of work-in-process inventory.

At Martin Marietta, as at many high-tech firms, most documents were written by technical or business staff. Usually, staff trained in technical communication or journalism designed and edited documents and supervised their production rather than wrote them. We collaborated with the writers by reviewing outlines and compliance matrixes; participating in planning conferences; suggesting strategies for text and graphics; obtaining boilerplate text and graphics; providing writing guidelines on large projects to increase consistency in style and content; editing drafts for technical staff review; reviewing drafts for content, focus, and specific details to support points; disseminating review comments; and scheduling and supervising document production activities.

Rarely did the publications staff or outside consultants conduct writing workshops. Technical staff were hired, in part, because of their proficiency in writing, and managers assigned experienced writers to work with less experienced writers on proposals and reports. Also, publications staff edited the writing of technical staff both at draft stage and the final stage, to eliminate writing problems.

Some proposal writing workshops were held, led by outside consultants who presented suggestions about writing, especially placement of key marketing messages. However, consultants focused primarily on helping staff identify the firm's qualifications to undertake the project, and state marketing strategies that would strengthen the proposal.

Most of the documents I edited were classified, and those that were not contained proprietary information; therefore, excerpts cannot be presented here. At Martin Marietta and in most high-tech firms, however, the review and editing process eliminates most of the writing problems that could be illustrated with short selections. High-tech firms vary widely in what they do and how they do it, but the publication process is similar across a broad range of firms, and similar challenges exist for the writers. The most significant problems in creating documents, which are discussed in this chapter, are largely organizational.

WRITERS IN HIGH-TECH FIRMS

Most writers are either communication specialists with degrees in technical or professional communication, journalism, English, marketing, or some other nontechnical field, or they are technical staff with a degree in the sciences, technology, mathematics, computing, and so forth. The trained communication specialists hired to create print and on-line documents are referred to here as *technical writers*. Most do not have the technical expertise to write sections of technical documents; they instead plan and schedule publication activities, assist the writers, edit text and graphics, and manage document production.

In some high-tech firms, most of the writers are not specialists in communication. Instead, they majored in engineering, chemistry, finance, or some other technical field, or they received technical training in the military. These writers, sometimes referred to as *subject matter experts*, write frequently despite their not having been trained to be writers. Various studies have indicated that professionals in these fields, especially managers, spend up to 40% of their time communicating, much of it working with printed documents. These writers, who may be skilled writers as well as experts in their fields, are referred to here as *technical staff.*

In high-tech firms, technical staff are hired for technical expertise, and technical communicators are hired to support them by helping them prepare documents. Technical staff are more scarce and earn more than communication staff. Therefore, it is cost-effective for managers to transfer as much of the technical staff's writing responsibilities as possible to technical writers who understand the subject matter well enough to write about it. This frees the technical staff to do technical work.

Technical staff not only earn more but are among the last to be laid off. However, communication staff have advantages that many technical staff do not. Although some technical writers are assigned to projects from their inception and work on them through their completion (sometimes a period of years), more writers move from project to project as needed. They collaborate with more people on different projects over a period of time than do the technical staff. For people who are curious about business and technology, as good technical writers in high-tech firms are, the opportunity to meet more people and work with different technological applications is attractive.

Technical communicators often have another significant advantage: They work with *people* most of the time. In high-tech firms, documents are produced collaboratively, and technical writers collaborate to prepare a document, not only with technical and business staff, but also with other publications staff. Their work brings them in daily contact with others, and for people who enjoy working with people (as good technical writers do), such work has advantages over the laboratory or design work many technical staff have to do.

Writers rarely have the opportunity to continue to revise a document until they are satisfied with it. Often they must stop work on a document before they think it is as good as they can make it and move on to another project. Most managers understand and are sympathetic, but they want the best work the writer can do with the time and help available. Managers are not interested in the idea that writers write to discover themselves, to become better thinkers, to develop as writers, or to grow as people, as college and university writing instructors are. They want documents written, as quickly and as well as the writers can.

One impediment to the study of writing in professional settings has been terminology. Technical and business staff define *writing* differently than writing instructors do. For technical staff, prewriting activities such as invention and other activities such as reviewing what someone else has written are not writing. To most technical staff, writing is drafting, and even though they may work in large teams on a document, they write alone. To them, the phrasing of ideas in words and the committing of those words to paper or computer memory is writing, and it is something they do alone. Because many technical staff have this restricted definition of writing, technical writers need to help some staff see that pre- and postwriting activities are an important part of writing as well. Similar confusion exists over *mechanics, usage,* and *syntax.* Technical and business staff do not talk about writing the way writing researchers and instructors do. Teachers and students need to be aware of that, and technical writers do too.

THE WRITING PROCESS IN HIGH-TECH FIRMS

At Martin Marietta, as in most high-tech firms, the larger or more important the document is or the more sensitive its contents are, the more writers collaborate on it. Major technical documents usually cannot be written by one writer. They require information from different areas, and technical staff are increasingly more specialized. Technology advances so rapidly that it is difficult to find one writer with the technical expertise to write all sections of a document. Also, few projects are so limited in scope that one writer can cover all the technical questions and problems. Sometimes each writer writes only one narrowly defined section of a page or two.

Although collaborative writing allows companies to assign sections of a document to the appropriate technical experts, it results in a jointly authored publication that must be edited to have one voice: the company's. The firm created the document, not the writers; they are not named but are recognized for good work.

In high-tech firms, documents result from a *requirement* that may be internal (from within the firm) or external (from a client, government regulator, media representative, and so forth). Most projects require documentation—progress or interim reports as a project is underway, and a final project report on completion.

The technical staff member in charge of a company project is usually in charge of all documents related to it. He or she is usually assisted by a publications specialist (technical writer), who helps plan the document, assists the technical and business staff who create the text and graphics for it, edits the text and graphics, and schedules and supervises publication activities.

Often, the technical staff member (the *book boss*) determines the staffing and scheduling needs and budget for writing the document. He or she manages the outlining, writing, and reviewing of the document, and is responsible for its success. In the case of a major proposal or project report, his or her career might depend on the success of the document. The book boss usually outlines the document, consulting with the technical writer regarding the content, structure, and format, but the book boss, an experienced writer, is familiar with the type of document, the subject matter, and the audience. The book boss assigns the writers, sets up the planning conference, and organizes the draft reviews by technical staff. He or she may encourage writers to follow a company style guide, but they are not responsible for consistency in style in the document. Consistency in style and technical details is the responsibility of the technical writer who edits the document.

Collaborative documents are more difficult to produce than documents prepared by one writer. Collaborative writing requires greater control over the development of a document, especially by the technical staff member in charge of the project and the technical writer in charge of publication activities.

WRITING PROBLEMS AND SOLUTIONS—ALL WRITERS

Writing in high-tech firms presents challenges that all writers, technical staff and technical writers alike, face sooner or later. Most of the problems can be solved easily if writers and managers anticipate them.

Writing for Different Audiences and Purposes

When students write for a professor, they can assume that the professor knows more about their subject than they do, and that the professor expects them to show how much they know about the subject rather than to inform the audience. However, technical staff often write for readers who know less than they do about their subject, and they try to inform the readers about it rather than show how much they know.

These important differences in audience and purpose make writing in high-tech firms and other professional settings different from writing in school. Some writers fail to recognize the differences, however, and try to write as they did in school. Because writers are assigned writing tasks according to their expertise, some slip into focusing on their expertise rather than on their audience. Some feel a need to establish their knowledge to promote themselves. Although they usually write for an audience that knows less about the subject than they do, they sometimes forget that and write over the heads of their audience. As a result, many writers who were successful in college are unsuccessful in their professional writing. Writers are more successful when they try to impress their readers with how clearly and simply they can present information the readers need.

Good writers in high-tech firms ask two questions about their readers: "How much do they know about my subject?" and "How interested will they be in reading what I've written?" Readers will know a little about the subject, a lot, or something in between. Readers may be uninterested, very interested, or somewhere in between. For example, company managers from a different division might read a report on a project about which they may know very little, but they might be very interested. Co-workers on the writer's project may know the project well but might not be interested in the report because they are already familiar with the project.

Similarly, writers need to consider their readers' responses and control the tone as well as the content. What can happen when a writer neglects to control tone is clear from the memo presented in Fig. 4.1, provided to me by an Eastern Michigan University student.

MEMORANDUM

TO: All Staff
DATE: January - -, 199-
FROM: J - - - D - -
SUBJECT: Tardiness

Yesterday over 20% of our work force was not at their job performing their task, including serving our customers. Today the figure stands at approximately 12%. If I were to ask each one of you why you were late, your answer probably would be traffic conditions due to the snow or rain. That excuse prompts me to explain a few facts to you. Snow is not a strange phenomenon here in this state. It is something that we have had to learn how to cope with over the years. The fact that an employee is late due to traffic conditions resulting from the weather or any other condition is clearly not an acceptable excuse. The remedy to all the nonsense excuses is to leave your home earlier when adverse conditions exist. In fact, many of you just barely arrive on time. As a result, you have a high probability of being late. I consider that to be sheer negligence.

You are required to be at your desk working at 8:00 AM. Socializing or standing in the coffee line at 8:00 AM does not qualify you as being on time.

Hereon, as a result of the tardiness being up so high over the last three months, regardless of the weather conditions, each person including managers shall be here at their desk and working on time each day. If not, disciplinary action shall be imposed on each individual in violation of this rule.

FIG. 4.1. Failure to control tone.

Writers in high-tech firms are encouraged to state their subject, audience, and purpose at the beginning of a document, unless the purpose is to persuade and the readers will not be pleased with the bottom line. Sometimes writers have trouble focusing on the bottom line early in a document because they tend to create a narrative account of the process that arrived at that bottom line. Or they try to include all their data, which overloads the document and obstructs its focus. A common task of writing consultants is to help writers identify the bottom line and place it in a prominent position—unless the bottom line is bad news.

In high-tech firms, writers have two audiences: a primary and a secondary. A document written for readers outside the firm will be reviewed by the writers' supervisor and perhaps other company staff before it is revised, put into production, and released to the outside audience. These reviewers are a secondary audience. The outside readers (the firm's customers) are the primary audience. When writers have two audiences, they must satisfy their secondary audience with the document while they try to make it communicate effectively with the primary audience. Usually, the secondary audience is familiar with the primary and can provide effective review. Differences of opinion are solved by the document manager, not the writers.

Writers working on a document often write different sections to be read by different readers. This is especially common on proposals. For Martin Marietta's successful *Supersonic Low Altitude Target* proposal, the same logistics engineers wrote sections of the logistics, safety, and testing volumes, shaping their logistics discussion to fit the marketing messages of the particular proposal volume. Whatever the type of document is, successful writers define audience and purpose, remembering the differences between the professional and the academic settings.

Gathering Information

When writers in high-tech firms need information, they do not go to the library, although most firms have a library or an archive. Instead, they interview people who have the information they need. Journalism students are familiar with such interviews, but many technical-writing students do not acquire experience—and more importantly, instruction—in interviewing. Planning is the key to an effective interview: identifying the right person(s) to approach; negotiating enough time; preparing clear, specific questions that elicit the needed information; having a convenient means to record the information; and keeping the interviewee on track. Some interviewees want to talk about their work instead of focusing on the interviewer's questions. Despite the time involved, an interview is a more efficient way to gather information than traditional research in printed documents, which writers do to prepare for interviews.

Writing Quickly

Writers in high-tech firms must be able to write and revise quickly, and switch from one writing task to another. Requirements for documents sometimes arise suddenly, and often there is little time between the first notice of a requirement and the deadline for the document. Even if there is more time to prepare the document, as on major proposals and reports, time is sometimes taken up by preparing drafts for a series of deadlines, especially in government agencies, as Joyce Magnotto (this volume) notes. At Martin Marietta, however, the successful *Multiple Launch Rocket System Terminal Guidance Warhead* proposal, which involved dozens of writers from four different countries writing over 6 months, had only two draft reviews before the final version was prepared.

Writers need to be able to define their subject, audience, and purpose quickly; gather information expeditiously; and write a draft for review quickly, without lingering over revisions or how the piece *sounds*, as it is only a draft for review.

Avoiding Pride of Authorship

Successful writers in high-tech firms learn to avoid pride of authorship. Their work is reviewed by technical staff whose task is to identify all the weaknesses in it, and some reviewers pride themselves in how critical they can be. Reviewers and writers often do not meet face-to-face to discuss the draft. Some reviewers tend not to be as concerned about how they phrase their comments as fellow students or writing instructors were. Some writers do not realize that most reviewers were never taught to couch criticism in positive tones. Some writers see criticism of their work as criticism of themselves; however, successful writers do not take criticism of their work personally. They expect reviewers to be as critical as they can, in order to help them make the final version as good as it can be.

In responding to reviews, writers make sure they understand the reviewers' complaints and suggestions. Writers often find that comments on their drafts are more substantive and insightful than comments they received from classmates. Generally, they make the revisions the reviewers have suggested, unless the document manager disagrees with the reviewer's suggestion. Writers do not invest themselves in their writing the way they did in stories or essays in school. Instead, they see their writing as something they are paid for doing, by someone who must be satisfied with what they write. It's a business arrangement: The writers—technical staff or technical writers—satisfy their supervisor, remembering that they cannot please all of the people all of the time, which was much easier when they had an audience of one professor.

Interacting in Small Groups

Although writers draft alone, they collaborate with other writers throughout the creation of a document, in small groups and as part of the larger document team as a whole. Sensitivity to the politics and personalities in project groups is important for writers, and much has been made of the need for understanding small group dynamics. In high-tech firms, the writers assigned to projects have reputations for being able to produce. Unproductive, difficult, or troublesome people are relegated to mundane tasks, transferred, or laid off. There is always some conflict and need for negotiation and compromise within writing teams; however, the writer's job is to write. If a problem in a group affects productivity, the document or project manager, not the writer, solves it.

Succeeding in the Organization

Despite recent efforts by high-tech firms to streamline their organization by trimming managers, there continue to be levels of middle management in high-tech firms. Even in the most successful high-tech firms, many middle managers do not know what their staff do and how they do it. This problem is more severe in high-tech firms because, as technology develops rapidly, knowledge becomes outdated faster. Writers as well as managers have to learn about technical developments as they work current projects. Often, the only solution is for writers to educate themselves by reading on their own time, outside work—as most successful professionals do. Many managers do not understand what is involved in a writing project, so they do not allow enough time, staff, and money for the writers to be able to do what they want done in the document. Consultants can help technical staff and technical writers clarify for the company managers what must happen and how much must be spent to create a document to certain specifications. In smaller firms, there is greater likelihood that technical staff need such help.

Another organization problem for writers in high-tech firms is having two bosses. Many high-tech firms practice matrix management, in which writers and other employees have a *functional manager* (their boss in their department) and a *project manager* (their boss on a particular project). A writer's functional manager controls his or her assignments and salary, but reports from the writer's project managers influence the writer's performance evaluation, on which annual reviews and raises are based. So both managers determine a writer's future, and he or she must please both, by collaborating well.

When large documents are produced in high-tech firms, different sections are put into production (typesetting, layout, printing, and so forth) at different times. Writers sometimes get anxious when production work on their section is scheduled close to the deadline. When this happens, experienced writers know to stay out of the way, but be available if needed. Inexperienced writers sometimes need to hear how important staying out of the way is, to meet a document deadline.

Another problem for less experienced writers is working on more than one, often several, documents at once. Writers are rarely assigned to only one project at a time. Matrix management allows staff to be assigned to projects as needed, using their time more efficiently. It is like a student's working on two or three papers at the same time. But the stakes—the job—are greater, so the writer has to make sure that each document is as good as it can be. To solve the problem, writers make use of free time to get ahead on work due later, as students do. Also, writers keep hard copy and text files of their work, so that they can recycle or adapt them for future documents.

Coping with Computers

In high-tech firms, just as in school, computers sometimes create problems; files are lost and systems can crash. Few students complete an undergraduate degree without losing an important paper—roommates or friends reformat disks, and viruses spread like viruses. In high-tech firms, where a system may have several hundred users, a web of networks, and overworked equipment, the problem is magnified for all users. Writers solve the problem by backing up their files regularly (never counting on someone else to), and copying their files to disks no one else has access to. Also, they find out who to call when things go wrong.

Handling Overwork

Good writers in high-tech firms get called on to do more and more writing because they are good. More project managers want them assigned to their projects. Sometimes, writers' supervisors do not protect them sufficiently, limiting their assignments to what reasonably can be accomplished in a 45-hour week, and some writers end up with more work than they can handle. They then have to choose to put in more hours or take work home to get the documents written well, or spend less time on each document, even though they know that it will not be as good as it could be. For conscientious writers, this *settling* can be stressful—as can working 60 or 70 hours a week, often without overtime or "comp time." At Martin Marietta, I was paid time and a half for overtime after 45 hours a week, on most projects; company policy regarding overtime is something applicants should inquire about during their second interview.

On important projects, stress and tempers can run high. A nationally known proposal consultant used to tell a story about a planning conference in which two managers got into a fist fight over a design issue. Such behavior is rare but understandable when careers are at stake. Writers can burn out, as other technical and business staff do. However, managers are usually operating under cost-containment agendas, and those managers seem more efficient to their supervisors (and are sometimes paid more) if they manage to get more and better writing out of their staff without paying overtime or hiring other staff, consultants, or contract writers to get the work done. Most firms that operate this way find that their writers make use of the revolving door and move on, now wiser, to write for other employers. There are always opportunities for good, experienced writers. One of the writers I worked with was in his third term of employment with the firm; he had quit twice to go to work for other firms (with a salary increase), but each time he was hired back (with another salary increase) because his skills were needed.

Creating Specific Types of Documents

In addition to the problems that arise on most documents, certain documents present added challenges. Annual reports, usually written by public relations staff or an outside agency, must sound positive and make the company look appealing even if the year's performance was poor. Interim or final reports on projects that have gone badly present a similar challenge: to accentuate what went well but downplay the problems. This is usually done by burying the problems toward but not at the end, in long paragraphs and long, complex sentences with passive voice and vague phrasing.

For many high-tech firms, major technical proposals present the greatest challenge. Before a decision can be made whether to spend the money to prepare a proposal for the contract, staff must determine the technical approaches the company will take for the research, development, or production work called for by the customer. Staff often begin writing before proposal guidelines are released and then revise as they interpret the requirements of the request for proposal. Marketing strategies must be defined and later worked into the proposal. The planning, writing, editing, reviewing, and production work often happens very quickly to meet the deadline for proposal submission.

High-tech firms want technical staff and technical writers to be familiar with common types of documents through experience or course work. They want candidates who understand the types of documents—why they are created, what goes in them and how, and who reads them and why. On writing projects, managers team up new staff with experienced staff to develop the new staff's writing skills.

WRITING PROBLEMS AND SOLUTIONS— TECHNICAL STAFF

In addition to the challenges all writers face, technical and business staff have some writing problems that are different from those that technical writers face. They primarily concern the writing process—what it is and how to use it in a collaborative setting.

Understanding Writing

Technical staff often have a different attitude toward writing than technical writers do, as they have different responsibilities. Their job is not to produce written or on-line documents but to design and conduct research, development, or production efforts to answer technical questions, manufacture a technical product, and so forth. Technical staff know that technical documents are important to what they do, but they entered their field not for the writing involved, but for the technical aspects of the work. Many technical staff recognize writing as necessary for funding of their work, but they tend to see it as something that takes time away from their work.

Some technical staff assume that they cannot *write* because they have trouble finding the right word, punctuating, or making their writing grammatically correct. Many staff do not distinguish writing from editing, and what they interpret as difficulty in writing is often a difficulty in editing well. Many technical staff had writing teachers who emphasized correctness in spelling and grammar without distinguishing editing from writing, so when they make mistakes they think that they cannot write.

Some technical staff fail to focus on prewriting and allow concern for correctness to interfere with their drafting. They have trouble leaving stylistic problems in word choice, spelling, grammar, punctuation, and sentence structure, as well as questions about the accuracy of details, for the revising stage. Clarifying the differences between writing and editing can help technical staff identify their strengths as well as weaknesses and improve their writing. Less experienced technical staff sometimes need to be reminded that no one gets it perfect with a first draft, so they should just write things down the first time and fix them when they revise. Then they more easily concentrate on writing down what they have to say, and it is easier for them to draft.

In most high-tech firms, technical writers or editors are available to help writers solve editing problems. In some firms, however, they are not, so writers do have to consider organization, content, and approach as they revise, and edit for emphasis, clarity, conciseness, and correctness in grammar, punctuation, and especially spelling *after* they write.

Technical staff who concentrate on writing, not editing, become more relaxed and less self-conscious about writing. Concern for correctness and precision does not interfere with their drafting. Many technical staff support the hiring of technical writers to edit their writing so they will not have to, allowing them to concentrate on their technical work while communication specialists make their documents more effective.

In most high-tech firms, technical writers are too busy to help technical staff with their writing, individually or in workshops. Writing consultants are sometimes brought in (at greater cost to the firm than freeing up technical writers) to help technical staff learn how to write effectively, especially for a general audience. Consultants are often asked to focus more on editing than writing, as Fred Reynolds, Joyce Magnotto, and Lynn Sadler (this volume) indicate. One common exercise is to ask the technical staff to rewrite a short document full of technical jargon in simple terms a lay audience could understand. This can be very challenging for technical writers lacking technical background and knowledge of the jargon, but technical staff can usually do it well once they see that their jargon is jargon.

Technical staff sometimes pay more attention to advice about writing that comes from other technical experts and business people than from technical writers. Professional and technical journals and general publications like *The Wall Street Journal* often contain valuable information about writing. At Martin Marietta, technical staff regularly brought me copies of such articles. Most apply generally to the writing technical staff do, but some are more specific. For example, instructions to authors are valuable for staff who write for publication in technical or professional journals. Although many journal guidelines concentrate on format, almost all have valuable advice on style and organization. Many technical writers build files of such articles and give copies to writers who ask for advice.

Writing Collaboratively

Collaborative writing allows firms to match writers with appropriate sections of documents, but it does present some challenges for writers. Because many writers are involved, they must define their subject carefully, organizing the material into narrowly defined sections. To avoid overlap with other writers' sections, they review the other writers' outlines carefully in planning or storyboard conferences.

Writers must take advantage of the few opportunities to review comments on their work and to revise it. Often the only chance writers have to check their edited and prepared text and graphics is during the review of the first draft. In some firms, early drafts of collaborative documents receive superficial or uneven reviews, so writers need to be able to search out useful criticisms. The technical writer should be able to help writers do this, as he or she has a better understanding of the entire document than individual writers who have focused only on their own sections. On collaborative projects, the number of people who participate in reviews is often restricted.

Writers usually want to see all the changes reviewers and editors have suggested though, and this is appropriate with a first draft. For later drafts, however, involving the writers in reviews or allowing them to review editorial changes might jeopardize the production schedule, as the writers usually want to revise further.

Some reviewers proofread for typos instead of making suggestions about content and organization. To generate more specific suggestions, reviewers are often asked to make additions, deletions, and changes on their copies, in order to make the draft read the way they think it should. One writer at Martin Marietta wrote on a draft of the executive summary of a major proposal: "Comments are appreciated but are not too helpful. If something is wrong, fix it. If something needs to be added, add it." Technical staff sometimes need help identifying effective reviewers, and technical writers are often called on to suggest reviewers who will examine the draft's content and organization effectively and make useful suggestions.

Collaborative writing presents challenges for a document manager (book boss) as well, including arranging for staff to write the document, managing the writing, enforcing schedules, and managing reviews and the writers' response to reviews. Staffing problems can become complex as writers are brought in from other projects, and monitoring the schedule becomes more difficult when more technical staff and technical writers are involved. On some projects, daily status meetings are held to identify *action items* (problems to be solved quickly) and to discover which writers must be prodded, assisted, or threatened. Directing the response to reviews becomes more complicated when review comments must be distributed to more writers.

For technical staff, the main challenge in preparing a collaborative document is juggling project responsibilities to find the time to write. For the book boss, the challenge is controlling the process, which gets more complicated as more technical staff, writers, and others are involved.

WRITING PROBLEMS AND SOLUTIONS—
TECHNICAL WRITERS

When technical and business staff write collaboratively, the type of collaboration varies, depending on the type of document, its subject and purpose, its importance to the company, the preferences or habits of the writers or the project manager, and other factors. On projects managed by a technical staff member, the technical writer becomes one of the collaborators, perhaps writing sections, editing the document, reproducing drafts for review, arranging art production, and scheduling, monitoring, and expediting Publications work. These different activities involve challenges different from those the technical staff face.

Planning and Managing Publications Work

Planning publication work on a document involves scheduling production activities, determining the staffing, and estimating the cost of production work. Such planning can be complex on collaborative projects, as staff from many different areas of the firm may be involved, working with other staff with whom they are not familiar.

Technical writers may have additional planning duties, including contributing to the document's design; writing or reviewing the document outline for content coverage, logical organization, and emphasis on key ideas or information; and providing guidelines for writers and editors. Writing and editing guidelines help ensure consistency in formats, acronyms and abbreviations, and technical details, to cut editing time. The technical writer often recommends usage guidelines or strict observance of the company style manual to the book boss, who decides which standards to follow in the document. In most firms, the company style guide is a reference, not a template.

The longer a document, the more important it is for the technical writer to coordinate activities with publications staff, letting them know how much work is coming, when it will be submitted, and when it is needed. Also, the longer the document, the more the writer needs to control its production. Often, he or she creates status sheets to do so. A status sheet can be as simple as a formal table with the document sections listed on the left and the production activities across the top. In one half of the box, the date the section entered the production activity is noted; in the other, the day it is returned. Status sheets can be very useful when a technical writer has several documents in different stages of production, as is often the case. A Gantt chart is also an effective way to monitor production activities. Such statusing is important because book bosses often want to know where each part of a document is at any time, and a good status or control chart can provide the answer quickly. Such control becomes essential when the document contains company-sensitive or classified materials.

The biggest challenge for the technical writer managing document production is getting writers to meet writing deadlines. The more narrowly defined and shorter a writer's sections, the less priority he or she might give them. Sometimes the writers concentrate instead on other projects they are working on; rarely are technical staff 100% dedicated to a particular project, much less a particular document. Therefore, the technical writer must coax material out of some writers, negotiate with others, and only rarely solicit the book boss's assistance.

Some faculty suggest that one role of the technical writer is to resolve conflict within writing groups. My experience suggests that this is not a good idea. Technical communication majors are writers, editors, or publication managers, not managers of the technical or business staff working in the group, and they should concentrate on doing their own job well. When they cannot because of conflict within the group or with a staff member, they attempt to resolve the problem by speaking first with the technical staff involved and, only if necessary, with the book boss. They stay out of disputes between technical or business staff and find that doing so enables them to work more productively with all the parties involved.

Editing

As most documents are written by technical or business staff, technical writers often serve primarily as editors. In addition to line editing the text for clarity, conciseness, and correctness, they examine larger aspects of the document such as content, organization, appropriateness for the audience, and fulfillment of purpose. Editing technical documents in high-tech firms requires some familiarity with the subject matter, as discussed later, but it also requires control, especially when the document is a long one written collaboratively.

When technical staff create a document collaboratively, there tend to be stylistic differences across sections—different voices. An important editorial objective is to make the document have one voice. Stylistic differences must be reduced to create a sense that there is only one author, as there indeed is: the company that produced the document. Such smoothing should be done by one editor, as he or she can achieve greater consistency than two or more editors can.

Incorporating Content Changes

All documents produced collaboratively—proposals, project reports, articles, manuals, and others—tend to come together at the last minute. For a technical writer managing production work, there is always the pressure of the deadline. Although some researchers have reported that publication deadlines in business often get moved up, in my experience they rarely change. If they do, they move out, not in, allowing more time.

Technical writers often have to process late content changes, especially when preparing computer documentation. The biggest problem in producing software documentation is having it ready by the release date. Changes to the software are sometimes made at the last minute, requiring changes in the documentation that delay its release. In most computer firms (where documentation is undervalued anyway), technical staff do not want to delay a release to allow the documentation to be revised so it is thorough and accurate. They argue that the documentation can be revised for the next release. This practice frustrates technical writers, but it does work. Users buy the software, and even if they have problems they cannot solve with the documentation or help screens, they receive help from an 800 number, buy a book on the software, or have a colleague help them.

Life would be much easier for technical writers in the computer industry if company officials valued documentation—but they do not. Therefore, technical writers who create user manuals are often frustrated, rushed, and sometimes forced to release a document that they know is not fully accurate. At the root of this problem may be the fact that many technical and business staff do not realize how much time and money it takes to create good documentation. In the future, downsizing in high-tech firms will reduce the number of staff available to support publication in general and documentation in particular. The situation will not improve until technical staff and managers understand how much time incorporating revisions takes. Consultants can help publications staff help technical managers see this.

Countering Reliance on Equipment

Technical writers in high-tech firms must adjust to changes in equipment brought about by technological advances. They keep up with developments in hardware and software for word processing, graphics, typesetting, and printing to see how these developments can help them do their work but also to determine what the equipment cannot do. Purchasing managers sometimes believe manufacturers' claims and commit money to leases or purchases of equipment without asking publications staff whether the equipment will solve problems and be fully compatible with what the firm already has. Publications staff stay informed about new equipment not only to take advantage of it, but to resist uninformed efforts to solve publication problems the wrong way.

Voice-activated computers, for example, have been touted as one of the latest time-savers in document production. Clearly, they will change the way communicators work. Writers have already found that when technical staff orally compose with tape recorders, there is often a clearer, fuller development of ideas and information, despite the pauses and false starts involved in dictation. Technical writers will have more text to read and edit, but there may be a more thorough discussion when technical staff compose on voice-activated computers. However, communicators will have to contend with the notion that because voice-activated computers put writers' work into preformed documents, the book boss will not need to do more than print out the file.

It is difficult to convince some people that computers do not solve writing problems. A new computer with more speed or memory can enable technical writers to run a program faster. However, computers cannot interview technical staff to get information needed for a document; they cannot organize the material; they cannot decide what to say, how, and why. Computers are merely a tool, but some firms seem more ready to expend capital for computers than to hire the writers they need to use them.

Managing Information

Many problems technical writers face are solved through managing information—acquiring it, providing it, or protecting it. Today, there is too much information being produced too quickly to sort it and determine what is important, much less assimilate it, store it selectively, and figure out how to access it. Developing technology allows more information on a disk—so if a disk is damaged or lost, more information is lost. As more terminals are networked, it becomes more difficult to control the data in a file because more people can access it. Also, writers find themselves having to remember multiple passwords. Many firms do not want clients, the general public, or even employees to have certain information. Controlling classified, company-sensitive, or proprietary information requires security procedures that technical writers must observe scrupulously: locking up materials when they are not being worked on, transferring working materials and finished documents with signed document control slips, and destroying drafts and working papers properly. High-tech firms and many of their clients require careful control of all information that could affect their competitive edge.

Writers need quick access to information, so many retain copies of company documents and duplicate text and graphics files for use in other documents. Many develop their own system of notes about where to find information about company products or services. Controlling the most important information—what other people need to know but do not—is often the key to job security for technical writers and technical staff.

Establishing Value

Another challenge facing technical writers in high-tech firms is demonstrating that their work *does* add value to company documents. In companies that do not produce written or online documents for sale, technical writers often have to justify their positions by demonstrating that their work does increase the marketability of the firm's goods or services. Although Martin Marietta was an exception, in many firms managers under pressure to control costs, not produce excellent documents, do not see the difference it makes to have technical writers work on documents.

Some technical writers keep samples of edited and unedited text and graphics, to show the difference their work can make. Sometimes, managers begin to see that communicators can add value to a product only when customers complain about documents, such as user instructions. In 1987, the revised IRS instructions for Form W-4 for withholding taxes were so hard to understand that public outcry about their incomprehensibility led the President to order hundreds of thousands of copies of the form destroyed and a revised, understandable form prepared.

The Society for Technical Communication has begun examining the *Value Added* concept in work by technical communicators. Their research may provide quantified evidence that trained technical communicators do add value to a document. For the time being, though, sometimes the only way to get managers to see the need for good writing, editing, and production work is to document what happens when weak documents are released. In my work, a writer who resisted having his writing edited had his draft printed unedited; when his manager complained about its quality, the writer was quick to seek editorial help.

Succeeding in the Organization

Cost Containment is the buzzword of high-tech business in the 1990s. Many firms try to control costs by controlling their salary expense. This sometimes means that there are too few staff for busy periods so that there will not be too many staff idle during slow times. In some firms, during peaks of activity, managers press salaried technical and publication staff into unpaid overtime, to avoid need for other staff for whom benefits as well as salary must be paid. As more and more professional staff become accustomed to working 50-, 55-, then 60-hour weeks, it becomes easier for cost-conscious managers to use this solution to solve staffing problems. This approach sometimes takes a high toll, but predictions about the job market in the United States suggest that there will be qualified applicants vying even for those positions in which staff are exploited.

One advantage for technical writers in hard times is that companies need documents written, and consequently they need writers. Publications specialists who work in high-tech firms and develop familiarity with the latest document production equipment have found and will continue to find that there are job opportunities with other firms that need documents created. However, available positions go first to people with significant professional experience and a background in the technology involved in the firm's work.

Another key to success in high-tech firms is establishing a good working relationship with other publications staff. Several discussions of workplace writing have examined how technical writers need to establish good relationships with business and technical staff. However, they must also do so with publications staff, who can be excellent sources of information about company documents, projects, and staff as well as valuable resources for getting jobs done quickly and well. Writers need the cooperation of publications support staff, and they earn it in several ways. They learn what it takes to do the work the support staff do. When they schedule work with support staff, writers are honest about deadlines and other requirements. They consult staff early on projects and keep them informed throughout. On completion of a project, writers make sure that publications staff are recognized for their work on the document. At Martin Marietta, publications staff—not just managers—were invited to the "win party" celebration for each successful major proposal.

Being Informed

There are differences of opinion about how much technical background technical writers should have, and about how familiar they should be with their subject matter, especially when they write for a lay audience. Some researchers have suggested that if writers know much about the technology with which they are working, it is more difficult for them to translate the information to a lay audience, to be an advocate for the readers. For example, on documentation projects, writers are sometimes assigned to the project from the beginning and become technical experts in the software. The argument states that it is then harder for them to produce good user documentation because it is harder for them to remember what the users of the documentation will not know. This is a dangerous line of reasoning, for several reasons. It assumes that technical writers have trouble presenting material at the appropriate technical level. Technical writers should not have any trouble writing for a general audience. The more they know about the subject, the more they understand, the easier it is for them to translate the information effectively. But it is difficult for writers to present technical material to lay readers if the writers themselves do not understand it.

Second, technical staff working with uninformed writers or editors are often reluctant to allow them to do much with their work. They fear that ignorance will lead to errors or weaknesses in the discussion, creating problems for the technical staff who wrote it. Because technical experts' reputations often rest on their writing, they want technical writers who assist them to know enough about the material to be able to help them, not just dot *i*s and cross *t*s. Technical staff very quickly discern a technical writer's expertise, and they are far more comfortable with communicators who are familiar with the technology. Technical writers with sufficient technical background to add value to a document are accepted more readily, trusted more fully, and given better assignments. Those who do not have such a background are sometimes relegated to proofreading.

If technical writers do not understand the subject matter of a document well enough to be able to ask technical staff the right questions when they gather information, they might not get the information they need for the document, or they might create an impression of incompetence. Also, writers without technical backgrounds find it harder to keep up with developing technology, especially the transfer of technology to other applications.

Clearly, no one can expect a technical communicator to have the same level of technical expertise as a technical staff member. Without some understanding of it, however, technical writers may be unable to clarify discussions of concepts or identify inaccuracies. Successful technical writers understand the fundamental concepts underlying the material. Technical staff are pleasantly surprised when technical writers know about and are interested in the technology involved. Technical knowledge and interest go a long way in helping technical writers gain the respect of technical staff.

Consider an excerpt from the Evaluation Criteria section of Department of Defense *Request for Proposal FO8635-84-R-0132,* for the design of a seeker for a "smart bomb" (see Fig. 4.2).

The passage illustrates the specificity of the instructions technical staff respond to, but it also illustrates the challenge for the technical writer editing the proposal, who must have some technical background to edit the document effectively.

Technical writers work with materials that range from highly technical discussions to nontechnical promotional and marketing materials. Writers without technical backgrounds prepare nontechnical documents such as

---

(1) The specific areas of evaluation shown in descending order of importance are as follows:
   (a) Technical
   (b) Management
   (c) Cost/Price
(2) Technical Area: The items and factors to be evaluated in this area are listed below, in descending order of importance.
   (a) Technical Area:
      1. *Seeker Design.* The offeror's proposed design must be technically sound and responsive to seeker performance requirements. The design must be in sufficient detail to provide the evaluators a basis for making an engineering evaluation.
      2. *Sensor Design.* The IIR sensor must be capable of detecting high value targets under a wide range of target characteristics, clutter levels, environmental conditions and employment scenarios. The sensor design shall be evaluated against detection range, minimum resolution, sensitivity, clutter reduction, field of view, and pointing accuracy.
      3. *Acquisition Capability.* The proposed seeker must be capable of autonomous detection and acquisition of targets from the given target classes with the given launch uncertainties. The seeker shall be evaluated against target detection and validation schemes, false target recognition methods, search uncertainty area considerations and weapon delivery flexibility.

FIG. 4.2. Sample request for proposal guidelines.

annual reports and some policies and procedures, and they coordinate the production of documents. But when that is all they can do, they are of limited value to a high-tech firm. Having a technical background makes writers more valuable because they can do more for their employer, and it gives them far more employment opportunities. Respondents to a survey about students' education for work in technical communication stressed the value of technical expertise; 70% of the respondents recommended that technical writing students study computer science, 40% recommended studying physics, and 40% recommended studying engineering.

The more technical writers know about the technology involved in a product or process, the more accurately they can describe that product or process. Technical staff sometimes give writers very technical material to create documents that are for a general audience. To write about technology, writers must understand it; they cannot write about a subject with which they are unfamiliar. It is detrimental to suggest, as some have done, that for technical writers ignorance of technology is preferable to knowledge.

IMPLICATIONS FOR TEACHING

Technical, scientific, and professional communication programs preparing students for the writing that technical staff and technical writers do in high-tech firms need to focus less on academic settings and more on the high-tech workplace. Students need to acquire basic knowledge of science and technology through course work. They need experience collaborating with students majoring in technology and business. They need experience with graphics programs and with interviewing. They need to consider effective communication strategies for multicultural and international settings. Above all, they need to learn to write, revise, and edit well.

Technical Knowledge

In high-tech firms, beginning technical writers are expected to have some background in scientific principles. Understanding technical principles can increase writers' confidence, improve their ability to present technical material, and help them learn about the field. Technical communication faculty should encourage students to develop a background in science and technology. Students with only introductory course work in a subject will not know enough about it to communicate information about current applications. However, students who concentrate their scientific study in one field may find it hard to move into writing in other fields. Prospective technical writers should master basic scientific principles such as those of physics or biology in courses beyond the first-year level, and study their application in different fields. Or they should follow a structured program of reading and videos. Incorporating writing-to-learn assignments in technical writing courses is a good way for faculty, as well as students, to develop technical knowledge.

Although some technical communication programs have a track designed for students with substantial backgrounds in science or technology, most do not. Most require one year in math or science beyond the freshman sequence—hardly enough to prepare students to present current technical information in that field. Teaching students how to communicate is important, but encouraging students to learn about what they will be trying to communicate is essential.

At the 1993 Society for Technical Communication annual conference, I asked job interviewers about students' preparation for work in technical communication; nearly all interviewers stressed technical knowledge. Their responses included such statements as "We're not going to hire any more English majors—they don't know anything," and "If writers don't know the technology, they can't be more than Kelly Girls."

Some opportunities in technical communication require a background in science or technology; some do not. Faculty should be able to help students identify both types of opportunities and discern what students need to take advantage of them. Students who want to work with technical materials, however, will increasingly be expected to have a technical background. At Los Alamos National Laboratory, a major in science or technology will soon be required for work as a technical writer. At Lawrence Livermore National Laboratory, course work in science or technology is considered critical for work in writing or editing.

One head of a large technical service firm told me, "We prefer to hire technical communication graduates who have strong writing, editing, and publication skills and have at least a minor (20–30 hours) in technical course work. We are looking for writers who have a strong affinity for and ability to learn science and technology." Increasingly, employers will want technical writers to have an undergraduate minor, if not a major, in science or technology. The field of greatest current interest is biology, given the expected growth in medical and environmental writing.

How might faculty determine which courses technical communication students should take to develop technical backgrounds? Talking with department heads in other majors can help, as can surveying area employers. Consulting faculty in other disciplines has another benefit: their support for scientific and technical communication programs increases.

Many technical communication faculty have limited knowledge of science and technology. That is logical; they are experts in communication, not calculus or metallurgy. However, many need to know more about communication outside of academe. Too few read *The Wall Street Journal*, professional journals in technical fields, *Scientific American*, or *Science* regularly, often because the time it takes to grade papers prohibits reading that does not contribute directly to a manuscript for publication. Keeping current on developments in science and technology is difficult, but faculty must do so to keep up with their technical students, and their clients when they do consulting work.

Contact with Technical and Business Students

In most technical communication programs, the upperclass technical or professional writing course has technical communication or English majors mixed with students from engineering, the sciences, business, and so forth. This mix is good, as science and technology majors get practice writing for a nontechnical audience and discover that what they are sure is simple and clear enough for a lay audience usually is not. Technical communication majors can find out from other majors about the work technical and business staff do.

In some programs, however, students are grouped by majors, and a section of technical writing may be all engineering or technical communication students. When the sections are homogeneous, students do not get as much practice writing for other audiences, and they do not get the valuable experience of working on documents with students in other fields. Their interactions with technical and business students, especially interviewing them to gain information needed for a paper and helping them explain concepts from their field to a lay audience, can better prepare them for working with technical and business staff in high-tech firms.

Computer Experience

Students considering work as publications specialists in high-tech firms need computer experience. Students need experience with a word processing program, a graphics program, and a desktop publishing program; which ones do not matter, as students who know one program can learn another quickly. Students should have experience on Macintoshes and IBMs or clones. Experience with Interleaf or Ventura Publisher is not expected in candidates for entry-level positions, nor is mini- or mainframe experience. If students plan to write computer documentation, they should be able to program in at least one widely used language, and they should have at least one course in systems.

Writing managers in high-tech firms expect technical communication students to have the tools for publications work; therefore, technical and professional communication programs should require students to use a variety of hardware and software. Some may concentrate too much on computer experience. Publications managers in high-tech firms want writing and editing skills above all, so instructors should not let computer experience take precedence over the development of writing skills.

Experience Writing, Revising, Editing, and Proofreading

A project leader in a leading computer firm once told me, "Our company has found that persons with degrees in technical writing cannot write."

Technical communication students will be expected to be strong in all the steps of the writing process. They will also be expected to emphasize the product, not the process, as the final document is what is important in high-tech firms and other professional settings. They need experience presenting technical material, not writing critical analyses of literature, formal essays, or narratives of personal experience. The traditional research paper on a technical subject can be valuable for teaching students about science or technology. However, technical staff expect beginning technical writers to be familiar with common types of documents—proposals, progress reports, manuals, correspondence—and few students will go on to write traditional research papers in their work. Technical communication programs should focus on these common types of professional documents, ensuring that students understand their purpose, formats, and rhetorical strategies. The assignments should provide experience writing and editing for different audiences, from lay readers to technical experts. Some of the assignments should be in-class writing to help students learn to write the "quick and dirty" first drafts they will be called on to write in their work.

My consulting and work experiences indicate that a technical editing course should be part of every technical communication student's program. Technical writers need strong global and local editing skills to restructure and reorient documents, to focus on key material, and to copyedit effectively. They will be expected not just to correct errors in grammar and punctuation but also to explain the errors and their corrections. Also, if they have learned about staffing, scheduling, and budgeting publication work, employers will give them more responsibility sooner, and the writers will advance more rapidly.

Proofreading is a crucial skill in technical communication, so there should be formal instruction in proofreading techniques for one-to-one and final proofs, after the students have mastered grammar and punctuation. Proofreading is often taught only as a final clean-up designed to catch typos, but instructors should teach students to proofread for such details as statistics, proper names, and sense errors. Also, students should learn how to help others proofread effectively, because when they are managing production of documents, they will not have time to proofread documents themselves. Using other writers' work, students need to practice the attention to detail that effective proofreading requires.

Publications managers and technical staff want technical writers who can communicate technical information; they do not care whether the writers know much about theory. To the degree that studying theory improves a student's ability to communicate technical information, theory is appropriate in professional and technical communication courses. Very few people in high-tech firms see any connection, however, between communication theory and creating professional documents. Students who are long on theory but short on writing skills will be at a disadvantage when they compete for jobs, so faculty should make sure that students get a balance of theory and practice.

Instructors should concentrate primarily on the students' writing. Examination of small group processes, audience analysis, and composing theory can help students prepare for work. They will be better prepared, however, if they are familiar with scientific theory and technical knowledge. The bottom line, however, is that they will be hired to write well. So while instructors examine theory, they must also be sure to provide students with substantial practice with the entire writing process.

Experience with Graphics

Employers expect beginning technical writers to be able to present information in graphic form, as graphics are common and important in technical documents. Students should know how to use a popular graphics program, but more importantly they should know principles of effective visual communication found in books by William Cleveland (1985), William Horton (1991), Edward Tufte (1983), and others. To be able to draw a bar chart with a computer is a useful skill, as is knowing how to type. To be able to construct an effective bar chart or to edit a weak one is more important, just as writing well is more important than being able to type.

As companies try to control costs, many cut back on support staff, including graphic artists and technical writers. Artists are often cut sooner than writers, as they are usually paid more. Writers who can take up some of the slack by designing and creating simple data or representational graphics are more valuable to a firm and less likely to be cut.

Except for technical communication students who want to work as graphic artists, it is not necessary that students know how to create orthographic or axonometric drawings or other complicated types of technical illustrations. It is not necessary that they be able to sketch or draw well, but it would make them more attractive to employers. It is important that they understand what types of graphics best present certain types of information, what types of graphics work well with different audiences, and what specific types of graphics should and should not contain to be effective. Also, it is becoming increasingly important that technical communicators be sensitive to the use of graphics for multicultural and international audiences. Icons must be designed carefully; the technical writer may know the audience better than the designer does, so he or she should check the designs to be certain that nothing offends the audience or creates a bad impression of the firm.

Specialization

As technical staff become more specialized, technical writers do too. Specialization is natural; as writers gain experience, they choose an area based on their interests and experience. However, specialization can be detrimental if a writer chooses an area without enough experience to be sure that it is the right specialization or knowledge where writers will be needed in the future.

Technical communication programs should be careful not to overspecialize. As programs encourage students to specialize at the master's or bachelor's level, in areas such as medical writing or computer documentation, some students concentrate their electives on course work related to that field and prepare themselves too narrowly for the changing job market of the future and perhaps for their own changing interests. Course work beyond the first-year sequence in a number of subjects prepares students for more opportunities.

Multiculturalism/Internationalism

High-tech firms are increasingly multicultural in their staff and international in their business. Technical writing students with advanced study of a foreign language offer high-tech firms increased sensitivity to another culture, people from it, and business in it. The Italian film director Federico Fellini once described a different language as a different vision of life. To be bilingual—to be able to speak, read, and write a foreign language fluently—is all the more valuable and valued. But being bilingual is not enough. International companies want employees who are *bicultural*, who are not only bilingual but understand the different cultures from having lived in them, and consequently can do business effectively in both.

Many international students in engineering and the sciences have English as a second language and are reluctant to take technical writing courses if they do not have strong English skills. Often freshman English was an unpleasant experience because instructors considered grammar and idiom in their grading. Some technical writing faculty operate this way, but they should not. Students majoring in technical fields—English as a Second Language students or native speakers—will go on to be technical staff, not communication specialists. Instructors should incorporate the basic difference between writing and editing into their courses and help these students focus on writing, not editing, so that they will face writing with less trepidation and have more success. In most high-tech firms, technical staff have technical writers to edit their writing, doing a better job of it than the writer could and sparing the writer for the technical work for which he or she really is prepared.

Students interested in working for international firms should also be familiar with developments in machine translation. Simplified lexicons have been developed to facilitate machine translation, and systems are improving rapidly. However, because text being prepared for machine translation is usually syntactically oversimplified, most translations need to be edited by a technical writer, the same way that a good editor needs to review the work of a grammar-checking program.

Interviewing

Except in journalism courses, students usually receive little formal introduction to interviewing. However, interviewing skills are important, and technical communication instructors should incorporate interviewing into writing assignments.

A useful assignment in technical writing courses is to have students interview professionals and professors in their field to gather information about the documents that these professionals write. The students then present their findings in a report. For such an assignment, the students identify people who would be sources of information they need, arrange to meet with each person, formulate specific questions before the interview, listen carefully and take notes, and incorporate the information into their own discussion of what professionals in their field write. The assignment can be followed by another in which the student receives more instruction in interviewing and has greater responsibility to determine what information he or she needs to obtain. Such assignments can help students prepare for gathering information later in their work.

Collaborative Writing

Collaborative writing creates different responsibilities for staff who prepare technical documents; therefore, teachers of professional and technical writing need to acquaint students from different fields with the different responsibilities. Students are better prepared for work on collaborative projects when they understand the different responsibilities required. Students majoring in engineering, the sciences, and business will write sections of technical documents, so teachers should design assignments to help them develop writing skills, especially in organization and strategy. Teachers should stress thoroughness, attention to specific detail, and logic in these students' writing. They should help the students develop the ability to produce material quickly, without lingering over grammar, punctuation, or other sentence-level concerns. They should help these writers learn to accept peer review of their work and to review others' work effectively.

For students majoring in technical communication, English, journalism, and related fields, who have more opportunities as editors or publication managers, instructors should design assignments that involve working with materials prepared by technical students. This is not to suggest that technical communication majors should be taught only to edit. In many high-tech firms, technical writers write entire documents or sections of documents. But on major technical documents, and on smaller documents that are very important or sensitive, the writers are usually technical or business staff, and technical communication specialists have other responsibilities.

In collaborative writing in high-tech firms, invention is rarely a problem, because writers write from their training and experience with the subject. Assignments in professional writing courses should focus on subject matter from the student's field. In high-tech firms, documents are pillaged for boilerplate and often plagiarized extensively in a manner that good writing students have learned to avoid or hide; students need practice working substantial borrowings into their writing. Technical students must practice focusing on a narrowly defined subject, writing to strict space limitations, and emphasizing key data or marketing strategies. Technical writing majors need practice in editing for consistency in format, style, mechanics, and tone, because editing becomes more difficult in collaborative writing.

Peer review and small group work are the most common pedagogical techniques to teach collaborative writing. They work well for many instructors, but their apparent simplicity is deceptive. Preparing students to be effective reviewers of content and organization, able to present valid, useful suggestions in a positive manner, is difficult. It takes practice, for the instructor as well as the students. Traditional instruction—having students write on their own for the instructor as the audience—does not prepare students for writing in which teams of writers, editors, and reviewers produce documents in an organization, just as having students write analyses of literary works or writer–centered essays in freshman English does not prepare students for most occupational writing.

One approach is group-writing projects in which responsibilities are distributed so that they match those the students will have on collaborative projects in their work. For example, communication students might plan and edit instructions for a graphics program, and technical students might write them.

Efforts to prepare students for writing in their work are complicated by a number of factors. Some are student-centered. Students who have not worked in business have little sense of the importance of writing in their fields, and it is hard to convince some students that they will need the writing skills that teachers try to help them develop. Having students write about what professionals in their fields write is a good way to educate and motivate them; when the students discover that they will have to write, they apply themselves more. Also, if teachers design assignments that invite students to communicate knowledge from their chosen field or major, they may expect information that many students just do not have yet, even students in advanced writing courses.

Some factors that complicate the teaching of writing are teacher-centered. Writing faculty often concentrate on rhetorical modes and traditional, teacher-centered assignments. Also, much research on writing does not help teachers develop classroom practices applicable to collaborative writing in professional settings, in which the audience is not a fiction. In the emphasis on process, many teachers have lost sight of the importance of correctness in a document. In professional documents, correctness is often the most important criterion of quality. Strangely, in my work in aerospace, nothing was objected to more strongly than spelling errors. Managers argued that spelling errors indicate that the document was not prepared carefully. They believed that readers who found spelling errors would assume that the document contained other errors as well, even of content.

In editing courses, students should concentrate on editing to a standard and editing for consistency. Consistency in format, style, mechanics, and tone is difficult when editors work with discussions written by many writers. Technical writing students need practice in achieving consistency in collaborative documents contributed to by several writers.

Perhaps the best way to prepare students for writing in high-tech firms is to arrange internships in nonacademic settings, in which students actually write sections of documents produced collaboratively. This is difficult, however. For the foreseeable future, high-tech firms eager to control costs will restrict the time staff have to supervise interns. Consequently, fewer students will be able to have the kind of internship that really introduces them to collaborative writing.

More and more technical and professional communication faculty are going into the workplace and finding out what writers in professional settings actually do. Also, they are discovering how the work force is changing as more women and minorities enter the managerial ranks. Continuing exposure to writing in nonacademic settings will help teachers understand writing processes in business and use collaborative writing effectively in writing courses, to prepare students for writing in their work.

CONCLUSION

In their writing in high-tech firms, technical staff and technical writers face several challenges. They must understand a document's subject matter, audience, and purpose to make it communicate effectively. They must work quickly and accurately. They must keep up with technical developments in their field. Technical writers must work well with technical staff whose knowledge, cooperation, and support are essential to creating good technical documents.

Technical communication work in high-tech firms has many benefits. Writers get to use their skills daily, collaborating with educated, intelligent people who value their services. Many technical staff are not confident about their writing and want trained technical communicators to help them make their writing more effective. For years, the ability to communicate effectively has been recognized as the most important factor in advancement for engineers and other technical staff. Most technical staff are anxious to have technical writers help them.

As technology develops, the material technical writers work with changes constantly. Most writers in high-tech firms look forward to working on different types of documents presenting different technical material; the variety makes their work more interesting, and the new material educates them. Also, writers develop knowledge and skills transferable to other firms in other parts of the country or world. For people who enjoy working with people, learning, and using their communication skills, work as a consultant or as a full-time writer in a high-tech firm can be very rewarding.

WORKS CITED

Cleveland, W. *The elements of graphing data.* New York: Rutledge, Chapman, & Hall, 1985.

Horton, W. *Illustrating computer documentation: The art of presenting information graphically on paper and online.* New York: John Wiley, 1991.

Tufte, E. *The visual display of quantitative information.* Cheshire, CT: Graphics Press, 1983.

United States Department of Defense. *Request for proposal FO8635-84-R-0132.* Washington, DC: Department of Defense, 1984.

United States Office of Technology Assessment, OTA-STI-238. *Technology, innovation, and regional economic development.* Washington, DC: U.S. Congress, 1984.

CHAPTER FIVE

Preparing for the White Rabbit and Taking It on the *Neck*: Tales of the Workplace and Writingplace

Lynn Veach Sadler
Human Technology Interface, Ink

THE COMPLEXITY OF WRITING AND OF ITS VENUES

What I present here is applicable to writing generally. I have never taught in a "professional writing" curriculum per se, and I am pleased to have had the opportunity to learn from my co-authors who have. We can import much of their teaching and findings into the traditional classroom and need to, for the majority of those who become writers in the workplace receive, at most, standard English/writing instruction at the school and college level. As people change jobs and directions more often, we who provide instruction in writing, which undergirds every career, must help. I believe that we should teach writing, overall, as a highly adapting human art that meets and surpasses circumstances. Bruno Maddox, in his review of Nicola Beauman's *E. M. Forster: A Biography*, voices one of my tenets: "The bottom line with both Forster and Ms. Beauman—what makes them such a great couple— seems to be a belief in the *effective use of the English language as the most reliable safety net life has to offer*" (italics added).

I am also pleased to have had the opportunity to reflect on what has evolved in my own writing and teaching of writing as I prepared this chapter. (I didn't just reflect; I sometimes had nightmares about "fitting in"!) From my experiences and from one of my writing workshop handouts comes the main part of my title. The appropriate excerpt from that handout follows.

129

Sample Macro "Seize-On" 2—Imprint and Prepare for the White Rabbit and for Taking It on the *Neck*.

. . .

In the days before writing and printing, when we were "oralists" perforce, our bards and poets functioned partly by the use of "formulas." Their works were highly "formulaic" but simultaneously individualistic and creative. Today's high tech world of boilerplate and your own world of personal macros that you have developed to save time with your regular writing projects, then, have, strangely, an affinity with that long-gone past. Modern jazz functions in much the same way: the musician is always prepared but leaves room for the unexpected, indeed anticipates the unexpected both in "reaching the groove" and "in the groove."

I hope many of us reach times when, for one little moment, we can do no wrong. The project comes together, the teaching hits the mark, the audience is with us, the writing is brilliant, and . . . . When I find that moment, I feel it as chills up and down the back of my neck. Taking it on my neck like that makes up for all the times I "take it on the chin" from others. I call it the Pym Syndrome. Barbara Pym was a British novelist who wrote mostly about old maids and small lives at the tea cup, but she has a character who *imagines suddenly having a white rabbit thrust into her arms.* I believe that writers and people in general have the right to expect experiences comparable to that—always possibility, always looking forward to the next whatever. Think about writing as preparing for your next white rabbit, for those "thrills" of the neck. Think about coming to work every day as preparing for your next white rabbit . . . . Remember, too: "If you build it, they will come" (*Field of Dreams*).

Perhaps I have some experiences different from those of the other authors of *Professional Writing in Context: Lessons from Teaching and Consulting in Worlds of Work.* My specialty is Milton, and I have a graduate "minor" in philology. Both resonate with the "high scholarly," and I have been known to quip that Miltonists are the "gorillas" of the scholarly set: People let them alone![1] I love footnotes, long sentences, puns, and marriages of "high-toned"

---

[1]Today, of course, Milton has fallen on bad times as one of the Dead White Males whom the politically correct set would kick from the canon. I'm also a knee-jerk liberal and have real problems siding wholly with or against political correctness. (To my amazement, the poem I wrote on the controversy and my difficulties dealing with it won "Honorable Mention" in the 1994 North Carolina Writers' Network Poetry Competition. It's called "Then Came PC.")

and "folk-toned"; they are part of my personality. I have taught traditional as opposed to professional writing at the college level; have published widely as an academic[2]; pioneered in computer-assisted composition (CAC) and established one of the first college microcomputer laboratories in the country to teach writing; and have extensive editing experience, which includes *The Computer-Assisted Composition Journal.* I continue to work, largely one-on-one, with nonnative writers, particularly with dissertations, journal articles, and books. I am a creative writer and blanch every time I have to let one of my characters commit a grievous (well, any kind of) grammatical error. I have helped establish my state's only Grammar Hot Line, which receives calls from all over the country, mostly from secretaries and CEO's, and promoted the weekly radio show, on the order of "Grammar Minutes," of one of my college's faculty. I also do a number of newsletters (e.g., for the local chapter of Habitat for Humanity) *pro bono.* The volunteers I work with on these projects, mostly retirees from the corporate world, are curious about every change I make in their copy. They want to know "why" and often respond with such comments as "Why didn't anyone ever tell me that sort of thing before?" They are very appreciative and very adept at what I call the "Eureka or Sudden Insight Syndrome" (e.g., "I see! That's great!" and "What a difference that makes!"). I also work with adults who just want to improve their writing, want to learn to write, or want to be a creative writer. They are generally seeking my services on an informal basis outside their job site.

I abhor "everyone-their" and "orientate" and still don't like split infinitives (though their derivation from our would-be Latin model calls them into question). I have difficulty "trusting" so-called professionals whose writing and speech are riddled with grammar errors. Yet I not only recognize but love language as a change broker. I know that writing is not fixed, that mine improves every time I edit it, that it can always be improved. As a writer and a teacher of writing, I have evolved and am evolving.

Likewise, my consulting experience may include some unusual venues. I have interacted with women's business clubs (e.g., Business and Professional Women) and professional organizations (e.g., in Executive Institutes for Organization Leaders sponsored by the North Carolina Council of Women's Organizations), men's business clubs and professional organizations, businesses, schools, and colleges. As a "scholar" president with a doctorate in English, I found myself functioning as something of a head editor for an entire campus—that "world of work" outside the classroom inhabited, for example, by office personnel, janitorial staff, and scholars-become-administrators. Companies are recognizing that their reputations, in

---

[2]Most would consider the distance between popular culture and Milton rather "wide," for example.

no small ways, link with the view of them in their corporate literature. How much more telling is the "literature" of an educational institution!

Business clubs and professional organizations tend to want modules on communications—not just writing but, as examples, "Conducting Meetings," "Public Speaking," "Grammar à la English Professor,"[3] "Technology and the Contemporary Executive" (including word processing, spreadsheets, data bases, spell checkers, and electronic mail), "Computers and the Professional Woman," and "Leadership." These titles suggest already the complexity of needs and the range of cultural change in not only "Worlds of Work" but their greater—and encompassing—"Worlds of Citizenship." "Writing" subsumes much that is non-writing.

Similarly, universities and schools are accountable, in business (and many other) ways for "outcomes assessment." They want not only "Writing across the Curriculum" but "Speaking across the Curriculum," "Reading across the Curriculum," "Values across the Curriculum," "Critical (Analytic) Thinking across the Curriculum," "Life-Long Learning across the Curriculum," "Student Involvement in Outcomes Assessment across the Curriculum," and "Creativity across the Curriculum." Also, along with businesses and government agencies, they want training in "Valuing Differences" and "How to Avoid Sexual Harassment." The U.S. Office of Personnel Management contracts for workshops and courses in "Basic Editing," "Effective English," "Essentials of English," and "Writing Techniques" and in "Leadership and Women," "Managing Organizational Changes," "Preventing Sexual Harassment," and "Managing Diversity." Writing (with speaking) is key in all of these.

Increasingly, then, my consulting and presentations have enlarged. I have wondered if this expansion acknowledges a perhaps unconscious cultural grasp of the fact that writing cannot be taught in isolation. In any case, in addition to giving workshops and presentations on writing and grammar (and variations thereon), CAC and computer applications to education generally, I work under the rubric of Collaboration for Quality (everybody emphasizes competition, but the real 21st-century skill is the transformation of competition and conflict into collaboration) and in the broader field of Total Quality Management and Total Quality Education, consulting with businesses, human service organizations, universities, and schools. One of the offerings, no matter the locale, is "Modeling for Quality: Speaking, Writing, and Doing." Others include "Senge and the Learning Organization"; "Beyond TQM (Total Quality Management): Competition > Collaboration"; "Management by Walking Around the Soft Side: Techniques for Motivating Quality"; "Valuing Differences: Avoiding 'Balkanization' in the Workplace"; "Process *and* Product, Qualitative *and* Quantitative: Wholeness and Synergism"; "The Necessity of Choice for Everyone in the Organization and Means of Providing It"; "Vision, Ethos, Mythos, and Credo: Locking on to Quality";

---

[3]No one has ever asked me for "*Writing* à la English Professor"!

"The Organization as Dinner Table"; "Learning Styles in the Organization: How to Recognize and Maximize Them"; "What Can You Expect of Employees, and What Should They Expect of You?"; and "The Transformation of Conflict into Collaboration." Writing (with speaking) is a leitmotif in each.

The springboard for my movement to collaboration is what I experienced in the CAC laboratory, a *writing* venue. Here is an excerpt from my presentation, "Collaboration for Total Quality Education," as Visiting Distinguished Scholar in the seminar, "Educational Leadership for a Competitive America," offered by the U.S. Office of Personnel Management at its Central Management Development Center in Oak Ridge, Tennessee, June 8–19, 1992:

> I have helped with and witnessed the kind of (societal, educational) transformation we need: in CAC (Computer-Assisted Composition; my coinage), the teacher "expects," the computer "enables," and the student performs. CAC enables students to produce a beautiful product, and the in-built revision process allows heretofore poor writers to achieve a sense of perfection or near perfection for the first time in their lives and in an area—written communication—in which perfection most frequently eludes them. Their writing skills increase; their attitude toward writing becomes positive. The effect is an enhancement of both qualitative (improved writing and vision of the self) and quantitative (increased and more accurate output). For years, we had a struggle between product and process approaches in writing: the traditional, quantitative way and the New Wave, qualitative way, respectively. CAC combines them synergistically. It can make the student aware of writing as process (prewriting to writing to revising/editing) at the same time that it enables the writer to have a measurable outcome, writing as product. CAC is an enabling, a self-collaborative tool that encourages the writer to become *writer and reader* or *writer and critic*, to combine what Peter Elbow calls the two *conflicting [competing]* skills required in writing: the ability to create and to criticize (*Writing with Power* 8–9). He concludes in the more recent work, *Embracing Contraries*: "I end up seeing in good writers the ability somehow to be extremely creative and extremely critical, without letting one mentality prosper at the expense of the other or being half-hearted in both" (142). CAC also encourages more traditional collaboration. Students at their computers talk first to their teachers and their Laboratory Director and then enter into dialogues with one another about writing, which becomes a communal experience. Finally, CAC is a "valuing differences" medium that can offer much modeling for the new kind of leadership and teaching we require: "In an electronic environment, the roles of teacher and student are radically altered, and cues of gender, age, and social status are minimized. What counts in such settings, as Michael Spitzer (1988) has observed, is the quality of a student's thinking. What is said becomes more important, at least for a moment, than who said it" (Selfe).

Almost everything I believe about writing is contained in that paragraph (overlong by workplace standards!). The observations I now add are germane to this book:

1. Never in the history of writing has the moment been more apt for rapport among educationplace, workplace, and *human/humane*-place.

2. We are not here to push writing/writers/people down but to pull reading/readers/people, including ourselves, up.

We are not "seizing the moment" in the world of work (or in the educationplace and society).

OBSERVATIONS ABOUT THE WORLD OF WORK

My experience in such world-of-work venues as those just described leads to eight global observations, most of which apply equally to the academic world. At the same time, I know that

---

Workplace   Writers

* write much more than they and especially their English teachers ever imagined they would.

* write collaboratively most of the time.

* frequently discuss their writing projects as they proceed.

* must write quickly and in the midst of noise and confusion.

* must have editing and revising skills.

* have to be responsive to readers.

OBSERVATION 1: THE LACK OF PLACING WRITING IN THE LARGER CONTEXT

How many writing workshops (or freshman writing classes) start with or *ever* mention why writing is important to the human condition, *is* the human condition? Participants and students are generally left to infer from what ensues that they write for totally practical reasons: to turn out impossible numbers of reports and memoranda in order to keep their jobs or to provide themes for a final grade. Who tells us that writing is entirely revealing, not only of our very selves, but of our views of and interactions with others?

Who helps us move from grammar to "valuing differences" and appreciating all parts of that continuum?

Who tells us that having difficulty with writing is natural because, as Peter Elbow has pointed out (*Writing with Power* 8–9), it involves two fundamentally opposed actions, *editing* and *creating*? To write is to "pat the head and rub the stomach simultaneously." We have to practice to get those two together in the first place, to practice more to overcome the jerkiness, and to practice more (and have something else) to rise to the level of art.

Who tells us that Plato considered a bed to have a higher order of existence than a poem *written about* (or a painting of) a bed because the bed was at one less remove from the idea of a bed ("bedness")? Who tells us that he warned of the loss of the entire classical rhetorical tradition if writing were permitted to dominate? Who tells us his objections to writing?

Plato's Main Objections to Writing (à la Ong)

— Writing is a static, "manufactured" product.

— Writing causes the weakening and ultimate loss of the faculty of memory.

— Writing is unresponsive to its audience, with whom it cannot interact.

— Writing lacks the "give and take" of speech.

More important, who tells us *that* and *how* modern approaches in writing, notably desktop publishing, are re-linking us with our classical roots?

If we are what we eat, how much more are we what we write (say) and how much more public the act! Writing is the most public of all of our acts. Speech is ephemeral; people will forget what we say unless it is taped and, even then, people are much more forgiving, at least of extemporaneous comments (except in the case of politicians speaking, of course). Who ponders such notions with us?

OBSERVATION 2: THE GENERAL FEAR OF WRITING (SPEAKING)

We may not address the larger context(s) of writing, but we often do encourage great fear of writing. Workers with a high school education or less, CEOs, and many PhDs outside the field of English, not to mention non-working adults walking around in the real world, evince a reluctance to reveal themselves in writing. We somehow intuit that being grammatically wrong is a high crime.

To offset fear of embarrassment, most people in workplace workshops want concrete, definitive, for-all-time solutions and protocols. They want the *Life of Right/Write* and this continuum, with "Rite(s)" the absolutes that make their writing correct and effective:

Wrong>>>>>>>>>>>>>>>>>>>>>>>>>>>>>>>>>>>>**Right/Write/Rite**

People demand from the writing trainer "tricks of the trade" that are miniatures of the plethora of how-to and self-help books on the market with names like *The Practical Guide for Writers, Apt Words and Forms for Apt Feelings,* and *Writing as Self-Defense.* They want to be told that the average English sentence has 18 words, and at least some of them, ever after, will comply with this "crutch for the efficient writer."

On the other hand, some writers could use a bit more trepidation about writing! We are all familiar with the Christmas letter that covers a year of family news and with the newsletters that professionals (e.g., dentists, doctors, insurance agents) send to their clients. But user-friendly desktop publishing software is spawning some amazing displays of writing, notably the newsletter my husband and I received from a car salesman. In the excerpts below, I have renamed his company FASTER and other automobile companies he discusses FAST, SLOWER, and SLOWEST. The cars assume aliases: "Poison," "Asp," "Midnight," and "Speeder." In actuality, *The CarBill* sports the name of its founder/editor.

The   CarBill

Excerpt   One

Timing is right to trade your automobile in.   We have a new line of FASTER product .I   feel it is time for me to start communicating with my previous customer   .This News Letter   will be the way   I keep you inform of all current change in the FASTER line.   I know that most people are busy   and do not have time to keep-up with all the changes.

Excerpt   Two

So, what the chance the Poison will develop into more than an auto-show curiosity , and make it into more than an auto-show curiosity, and make it into showrooms someday? Not especially great. Though FASTER has a recent history of getting show cars into production, Burke admits the Asp did. Its chance of making the production cut aren't even as good as those two other FASTER prototypes the Asp coupe and the Speeder think in term of 6000 cars at a price point like .More like 100,000." that , plus the industry relative inexperience in stamping and welding car bodies in aluminum, would make the Poison's start-up investment very high.And with it , the likelihood of an ultimate thumbs-down.

Excerpt Three

But the look is still a surprise. Like it or not,you have admit it's adventures. And for a car from a division notorious for its recent conservatism, that's a real departure. Under the skin SLOWER's new R-platform.which is also the basis of FAST's Midnight, despite insistency by FASTEST's team hat "only the floor,the carpet, and clearly share common to both cars." that 's trifle disingenuous, because the two cars clearly share common technology. For example , both have large box-section roof rails for extra body rigidity, and both boast a natural frequency of 25 Hz. Meaning,they' re are stiff as a SLOWEST F320.

Excerpt Four

Right buy American automobiles to keep this country strong.I know the issue that come-up it's quality. The American manufactory have receive a wake-up call. If you look in the consumers report magazine you will find what I'm saying is the truth . You know that in some country they do not allow our product to sold. American jobs depend on you patronizing American products. You are free to do send your money just think about how that came about?

Do we laugh or cry? We witness good old American entrepreneurship, creativity, daring, a feel for audience/customers, street smarts. . . . Actually, I'd like to offer my services; doubtless, all of the authors of this book would. The proud editor's company could use a writing specialist on call—well, writing specialist on E-mail. Excerpts Two and Three, "borrowed" from company literature, are especially good examples of the need for minimal editing skills.

I estimate that 95% of the freshman composition courses in this country receive papers with many more problems than those in *The CarBill.*

OBSERVATION 3: FEAR OF ORGANIZING
OR OF APPEARING TO ORGANIZE WRITING

I understand the fear and uncertainty generated by thoughts of having to write. On the other hand, I have been thoroughly shocked by the seeming inability to organize. People reporting to me as the CEO of an organization often appeared incapable of laying out their I, II, III, IV; A, B, C, D; and further subsets. Here stood a scholar with a lot of writing on her résumé at the helm. Could they have been afraid that I would consider their "breaking writing into pieces," as in an outline, nonintellectual?

Prior to that experience, when I was a Vice-President for Academic Affairs, I generated a short form (based on Milton's view of choice!) that my team and I could use in making "decisions with major impact." I was after a way of marrying philosophy and form (and, of course, of marrying my discipline with the new directions my career had taken). I used it myself in the new situation and encouraged team members to speak from it when they brought ideas to Administrative Council meetings for discussion and write to it in feasibility studies and follow-ons. The form looks like this:

Decisions with Major Impact

Decision to be made:

Date by which the decision must be made:

Alternatives:
1.

2.

3.

```
4.

5.

?

Which   alternative   is   best   for   the   institution?


Which   alternative   harms   the   fewest   people/areas?


What   is   the   decision?     Why?


Who   should   know   about   the   decision?


Who   will   disseminate   the   decision?
```

Similarly, I entered my early consultancies anticipating that the writing would be "skinny" (two or three skimpily-filled-out points labeled *1* and *2*). How was I going to teach the art of subtle elaboration? Again, I was WRONG. The writing was "fat" and "puffy." I had difficulty cutting to its heart.

My experience is apparently not unusual. I was recently in the second Carolina Publishing Institute at the University of North Carolina-Chapel Hill (May 31–June 17, 1994). Several editors involved with nonfiction, particularly those who acquire and edit manuscripts, spoke often of their difficulty getting writers to "break out" their points.

As Fred Reynolds suggests elsewhere in this book, when workplace writers "bloat" and "overwrite," they may be looking for beauty or striving to appear intellectual. Does a one-two-three-four approach "feel" over-simplified? Does dressing a point in verbiage enhance the point's importance?

OBSERVATION 4: WRITING BAGGAGE: LOVE–HATE MEMORIES OF TEACHERS

Many of us swear during and/or at the exit from high school or college that we will never write again, and most of us lug about an emotional suitcase crammed with writing memorabilia. Writing trainers can put them to good use. One strong memory is of being forced to tease out the "spoor" of the red pen.[4] Writing is THE preeminent love–hate medium, and those of us

---

[4]Many feel that computer programs allowing writing teachers and writing trainers to comment on material with standardized macros, as well as original comments, offset the "red-flag-in-

who make our livings by it probably enjoy most the sense of relief when the current project is over.

I have seldom given a workshop or talked to groups about writing (communicating) without at least one person raising a hand to share an anecdote about a former teacher, usually from grade school days. The speaker admires Miss (as was usually the case) Teacher because she "knew her stuff."[5] The rest of us in the audience infer that Miss Teacher was wonderfully strict, hard-nosed, and dictatorial and never suffered fools gladly. All of us sigh inwardly at the thought that such days and such people are gone forever. The lull of reverie is quickly shattered by an angry person jumping to his (often) feet to express deep resentment because different teachers, equally assured that they were right, gave different prescriptions for writing perfection. "And if the so-called experts can't agree and have nothing to teach, what are we doing here anyway?"

I surreptitiously pinch my arm to remind myself not to remind this person of how I started the presentation/workshop: emphasis on TOLERANCE, to wit—

with (charming, well, to me) tales of my own *childhood* mistakes (e.g., "*Yose*-mite" rather than "Yo-*sem*-i-te" Sam, "Ni-a-*ga*-ra" rather than "Ni-*ag*-a-ra").

with (charming, perhaps, but less than to me) tales of my own *adult* mistakes (e.g., this misuse of *hopefully* in the worst possible place: "Hopefully, some of the infelicities in those earlier articles have been corrected in the book.") I have just about eradicated *hopefully* from my vocabulary!

with the "fact" that, in the 18th century, the use of the apostrophe was often the opposite of ours—was *its* as "it is," *it's* as the possessive.

with the interchanging, in the 17th century, of *then* and *than* and my stewing over whether to use the authentic version of the Milton quotation—"to create/Is greater then created to destroy" (*Paradise Lost* VII.606-07)—on the cover of one of the journals I founded and edit, *Small College Creativity*; doing so; and never having been questioned but once at the now solecistic use of *then*.

with the fact that Shakespeare, along with many other great Renaissance figures, could not spell his own name!

with the quick explanation of why people have so much trouble with the principal parts of verbs (referring to them sometimes as "*principle* parts of

---

front-of-the-bull" (a great if wicked pun, *n'est-ce pas?*) problem of the red pen. Writer (and teacher) Doris Betts must spend hours producing her beautiful, calligraphic comments on student papers. I prize every such postcard and letter from her. However, I find the red highly practical; I can see it quickly and easily. When I edit my own materials in hard copy, I am uncomfortable unless I have a red pen in hand.

[5]Well, what do I, Ms. Self-Righteous, admire? See Appendix A. I was pleased to find the references to writing.

verbs"), as in *grow, growed, growed* rather than *grow, grew, grown.*[6] We belong to the Indo-European family of languages, whose verbs were "strong," thus forming their principal parts after the fashion of *fly, flew, flown.* Eons of time later, however, we found ourselves grouped in the subdivision of Indo-European known as "Germanic." One of its characteristics is "weak" verbs (e.g., *play, played, played*). Today, when we are so much closer in time to the Germanic period than the Indo-European, the pattern that predominates, naturally, logically, is the weak. When people use *growed*, they are responding to that dominant pattern.[7]

with the quick explanation of why people "reinvent" *you* as *you-all, yawl, you'uns, youse guys.* . . . Here are our modern personal pronouns:

	Singular	**Plural**
First Person	I	We
Second Person	You	You
Third Person	He, She, It	They

In earlier periods of English, each was distinct. Now, the second-person singular and plural have "fallen together" as *you*. Speakers/Writers who expand the *you* are trying to address and redress that loss of distinctiveness.

Instead, I point out that standardization "within house" is an achievement devoutly to be hoped for and that his own company has a style sheet for its public materials. Having recently participated in that publishing institute mentioned earlier, I could also now share that, as freelance copy editors well know, every publishing house has a different style manual and, thus, virtually every editing project they undertake requires internalizing a different set of editing guidelines.

Here two other opportunities jump forth also:

1. to declare that companies often provide writing training, not because they consider their employees dummies, but because they need to initiate them in the "house culture" and/or changes in it.
2. to point out, as in the seven *with* examples just provided, that, despite the tendency of writing to want to remain at the level of "art" rather

---

[6]If I am really full of myself on that particular day, I seize the "teachable moment" and, in today's language, "pull a sidebar": "I could but don't say 'the reason people say *growed* is because,' but that usage would be another grammar error. *Is* is (smile) a linking verb. It must have a complement or completer equal to the noun/pronoun it seeks to 'link' or 'match.' Hence 'the reason is *that* . . .'."

[7]My audiences have seemed to like getting such a "substantive" explanation. However, when I was in graduate school at the University of Illinois, the fashion was to teach freshman composition by having the students read a collection of philological/history-of-the-language essays. This practice was abandoned.

than becoming "science," even most of our "errors" are logical historically.

As to the old complaint that, if nothing is definitive, we have nothing to
teach, I will be adding another cherished piece gleaned from the Carolina
Publishing Institute. Its highlight was Reynolds Price, in the Marketing seg-
ment, speaking on "Book Marketing and Promotion from An Author's Perspective." In an aside, he mentioned his experience teaching one literature
and one writing course a year at Duke. In the writing classes, he prepares
the assignments along with the students, and they get to critique his work
as he critiques theirs.[8] He went on to say that teaching writing is comparable
to coaching athletics.[9] That is, the *skills* of a particular athletic event can be
learned, but not many who learn them will become a Michael Jordan. His
caveat was really for the skills part. The skills of writing (athletics) can be
learned if the would-be writers (athletes) are working with professionals,
are treated as professionals, and are expected to act like professionals.

I am pleased to report that the same view of professionalism and skills
undergirds the computer-assisted composition program, *Diagrammatic
Writing Using Word Processing*, I co-authored with Dr. Wendy Tibbetts
Greene as co-writer and Dr. Emory Sadler, my husband, as programmer.
The Preface includes the following:

TO THE WRITER

Professional writers are organized and imaginative. You may be surprised to
know that they think of themselves not only as writers, but as editors, critics,
and readers. In addition, they view the act of writing both as an activity with
a specific goal (a product such as an essay) and as an ongoing process in
which editing and revising play a major role.

Professional writers consider revision a fact of the life of writing. Please
consider yourself A PROFESSIONAL WRITER. *Diagrammatic Writing* provides
the discipline of structure and encourages creativity and expansiveness.

. . .

You can develop more than the requisite three body paragraphs, and you
will find creativity and variation among the sample essays.

---

[8]See Hunter: "I write the exercises along with the class (Creative Writing), sharing my
roughest work and encouraging an atmosphere in which others feel free to do the same."

[9]I'm no jock; I've even been "mean" on occasion about the ineptitude of that masculine
metaphor of the "level playing field." Nonetheless, like Reynolds Price, I find athletics apt.
Former Boston Celtic star Bill Russell offers the best support I know for moving from competition
to collaboration. See my "Collaboration for Total Quality Education."

Diagrammatic Writing also leads you through the process of constructing the nine different rhetorical modes standard to essay/theme writing. With the structure for each mode securely in your mind as a backdrop for demonstrating your own creativity, you will find your contentment while writing increasing apace. *Diagrammatic Writing* (and the computer) will make writers already comfortable with their craft more efficient.

OBSERVATION 5: THE GREAT WRITING DIVIDE: "LOFTY PROFESSOR" VERSUS "FRIENDLY NEIGHBOR" WRITING

Writing in the workplace is apt to be much more single-minded and at peace with itself than writing in Academe and its adjuncts. I still remember the difficulty Dr. Wendy Tibbetts Greene and I had "rewriting"—rewriting to the nth degree—an article ("Computer Applications for Writing: The Computer-Assisted Composition Movement") to suit the editor of *ABACUS: The Magazine for the Computer Professional*. As recently as July of 1994, the editor of the Book Page of an alternative newspaper in Virginia, while inviting me to become a contributor and reviewer, demurred:

> Before you say yes, let me warn you of two ways you'd have to lower your standards: you'd have to adopt a casual, yuppie-journalist writing style, and you'd have to expect our editor-in-chief to make editorial changes under your byline without your permission.
>
> Sometimes I have a tantrum when I see how he has rewritten my perfect sentences. But—that's journalism, as my reporter friends remind me. It operates under its own set of standards.

I can (and have always wanted to and meant to) be a scholar and a *real* person; so can many people. In our society, that approach is difficult, even in the days of "I'm O.K.—you're O.K." I can still remember returning, PhD in hand, to my small Southern hometown. Walking around with my mother, I discovered that I had become invisible. People tended to talk to her and to look at her, never at me. I always point out in workshops that the "ivory tower" is a cliché "to be eschewed"—and grin. Despite my good intentions, the cliché persists. Now, in the heyday of such scholarly phenomena as deconstruction and political correctness, it is rampant in the charges of those who see the campus as mini-war zones of professors turned in on themselves writing for the few they deem to be "their own kind."[10] Academics are at

---

[10]As Joyce Magnotto suggests in her chapter, this volume, "bureaucratic" writing gets even shorter shrift; few are willing to believe that it wants to communicate.

war with other academics, as at my own undergraduate institution (Duke); and the National Association for Scholars is probably amazed at the groups with which it gets linked.

During a presentation at the Carolina Publishing Institute by Neil Patterson Publishers, which produces science texts for colleges, one of the speakers, a science professor who writes for that house, told the audience: "When you're writing, *explain*. Don't just *mention*. English classes don't teach you that." He went on to hypothesize that the reason probably has to do with the fact that "English people" write about "material" that is "non-data-driven." A graduate teaching assistant completing her doctorate in Medieval Literature at the University of North Carolina-Chapel Hill later complained to me about his charge. She and her colleagues are now assigning "real-world topics" (topics they will use in the world of work?) to students.[11]

Ingrained in us is a sense that certain kinds of writing, even when we rail against them, are inherently better or "higher." Against his vein and inclination, Milton turned, for some 20 years, to the question of England's liberty in the prose tracts that he designated the work of his "left hand." They may have served the needs of his nation, but he reserved his poetry for his "right hand." Today, poetry is even further removed from ordinary people than is scholarly prose—the writers of both nonetheless inspire awe.

Stereotypically, the business world laughs at academics as impractical and lacking in common sense. Similarly, the academic world disdains the business world and pays little more than lip (printed page?) service to the business world's needs. College literature may set forth "preparing students for the world of work," but we all know that, too often, a hidden agenda is to turn out liberal arts generalists who appreciate the higher order of existence that has nothing to do (too many feel), with the world of work in which most of us live most of the time. Appendix B is an excerpt, "Making Business Palatable to the Academic World," from the keynote presentation, "Total Quality Management: The Issues of Change," that I gave at "TQM and Education: A Conference for the Community College System of North Carolina" (Southwestern Community College, April 19–20, 1993). It will indicate why I believe the moment is so right for bringing the two worlds together.

For some time now, I have found great compatibility between total quality management and education ("Some Recommendations," "Genial Iconoclasm"), and my particular niche in the movement is collaboration rather than competition. Again, my interest grew from the collaborative atmosphere that develops in the CAC laboratory. So much of what I have come to believe about the computer as a tool, an enabler that makes constant improvement possible because it eases the drudgery of writing, rings with parallels in the Total Quality Movement, for example, empowerment; choice; ethics; short-term

---

[11]As described in this book, Carolyn Matalene moves her students even further by linking "real-world" assignments with long-term citizenship.

solutions building to long-term writing practices; pride of workmanship; jettisoning of "quotas" (that is, getting rid of allowing x number of errors for a passing grade); a real spur of creativity; the needs of the customer or audience; the breaking down of barriers between departments (that is, the collaborative atmosphere); driving out fear, writing anxiety, and writing block because revision is not only easy but encouraged; revision as a fact of the life of writing; constancy of purpose toward the goal of improvement; participative management; the student as leader/manager of his or her own writing.

I am unaware of any writers in the workplace connecting Total Quality, originally a business concept, and writing,[12] and I know of only one other English teacher who has done so. David H. Roberts, of Samford University, in an essay called "Writing: A Process that Can Be Improved," has applied Dr. W. Edwards Deming's Fourteen Points for Management Transformation to writing, pointing out that the Deming philosophy of manufacturing as a process parallels the current focus on writing as process. As American industry got into trouble because it inspected the final product and fixed the defect or rejected the product, without seeking the underlying causes and changing the system that produced them, we in English focused on the writing product or, principally, on its errors, and did nothing or little to improve the writing process. We do not do so any longer, even if we have never heard of Total Quality Management or Total Quality Education!

Business has become tired of waiting for Academia to change and blames schools and colleges for the fact that the work force so often appears illiterate. Although business leaders decry the "dumbing down" of America, too many of them conspire with this process internally. One of the saddest pieces of information I have acquired recently is the latest approach to offsetting illiteracy. Corporations are hiring in-house writing specialists to teach managers and others to avoid formal writing and aim for the *4th-grade* reading level of one of every eight working adults in America. "Friendly Neighbor" writing, my generic term for what appears in different venues under various labels, is touted in the workplace, implicitly at the very least, as the opposite of the "Lofty Professor" writing we learned in school. "Friendly Neighbor" writing spins from "Dumbing Down," that chicken-and-egg phenomenon not just in our schools and colleges but in the real world in general.

Writing down to one's audience cheats the subject matter no less than it cheats both writer and reader. "Adulteration" is adultery in the marriage of writer and subject, and it applies as much to our adults as to our children. Writers have an obligation to meet the demands of their material; readers have an obligation to rise to the results. Milton is not easy reading, but the reader who engages with him finds balance and beauty as well as wisdom.

---

[12]According to Joyce Magnotto, the General Accounting Office is now applying TQM principles to writing and review processes, with the goal of reducing the number of review cycles while still producing documents quickly.

Although many of these trainers have been hired for their English majors and background, they make statements such as these:

- I designed this course with today's business writer in mind.

- Business writing is different from the academic writing we learned in school.

- Our [company] writing needs to be faster and easier.

- We're going to learn "Friendly Neighbor" writing. It has new ideas and techniques.

In times when even "Big Blue" has drastically altered a lifetime of policies and approaches, companies feel compelled to make customers understand their services and value. Many now publish newsletters aimed at persuading the readers to continue as or to become customers because of safety records, public service, value added, product or service quality, efficiency. . . . What has happened to the "persuasive essay" we still teach in schools and colleges if such efforts are "new ideas and techniques"?

The writing specialists at some of our major corporations promote

℞ short, simple words. [Company writers must avoid, as examples, *represents, sufficient, consequently, approximately, correspondence, the following, assistance, regarding,* and *forward.*]

℞ sentences that average 10-15 words. Writers should "worry" about sentences longer than two typewritten lines; a sentence with as many as thirty words will lose or at least confuse most readers.

℞ paragraphs with a maximum of six typewritten or computer-written lines.

℞ personal pronouns.

℞ active voice.

℞ the avoidance of Latin terms (*via, etc., e.g., per, et al.*), which "do not mix with American Business English."

℞ positive and pleasing words and tone.

℞ writing the way one talks.

To insure that their "prescriptions" are taken, at least the large companies have their writing trainers oversee regional pattern letter projects, apply readability scales, and run grammar readability analyses, not only on their public materials (e.g., annual reports, the "President's Message"), but on the memoranda of middle managers.

"Dumbing Down" may have been encouraged by readability scales and text-analysis programs, which were fostered by the corporate world,[13] but it is now in the soul marrow. The result is "Writing at Impasse: The Divided and Distinguished Worlds of 'Friendly Neighbor' and 'Lofty Professor' Writing"—bipolarity rather than continuum. Until we recognize the larger human arena both inhabit, raise expectations about writing in the workplace, and increase understanding of the interplay of audience and writer in the schools and colleges, we remain at impasse.

OBSERVATION 6: LACK OF APPRECIATION FOR WRITING AS A VISUAL CONSTRUCT

Given my observation of workplace difficulty with organizing, I should not have been caught offguard by an equally intense and related problem: inattentiveness to the way writing is placed on the page and to aids that enhance the grasping of meaning. I was stunned; I expected the work world, particularly in increasingly high-tech arenas, to sacrifice the verbal to the extra-textual features (e.g., headings, subheadings, white space, boxes, graphs, tables, figures, pictures/graphics, fonts, pitch, footers, headers) offered by CAC and desktop publishing.

Designers have applied "form as meaning" for a long time. So have poets—and not just those who write "shaped verse." Maybe e. e. cummings was the poor English teacher's version of CAC and desktop publishing. Yet, only with their arrival have we in writing paid much heed to the fact that structuring can not just enhance meaning but *be meaning* or *mean*. This stance has still not penetrated traditional writing classes. There we continue to accept (though, surely, grudgingly) hand-written papers and often present our own cursive to department secretaries who curse and translate it into syllabi and scholarly papers. We know that we can be beguiled by the professional look of word-processed papers. Do we consider the opposite effect of the aging notes and poorly copied handouts we often bring to class? We tell ourselves that computers; word-processing packages such as *WordPerfect, Microsoft Word,* and *Ami Pro,* which offer some desktop-

---

[13]Among the corporate text-analysis programs are AT&T's *Writer's Workbench*; Westinghouse's *Writing Aids System*; the Navy's *Computer Readability Editing System*; IBM's *EPISTLE* and *CRITIQUE*; and, more recently, PC-based imitations of *Writer's Workbench* (e.g., Aspen's *Grammatik II,* Decisionware's *RightWriter*). Text analysis programs continue to be developed, and they remain one of the most controversial writing tools.

publishing tools; and desktop-publishing software (e.g., *PageMaker, Ready-SetGo, Personal Press, Publish It!*) are too expensive and that such matters have little to do with *real* writing. We are, of course, unfamiliar with layout and typography.

I came early to computer-assisted writing and remain impressed with its results. Now, remarkably (and wonderfully), theorists in textual writing (particularly Fred Reynolds, "Computer-Assisted Composition: A Classical Interpretation," with his students, Gilstrap, Panetta) are arguing that desktop publishing can reconnect us with our roots in the classical rhetorical tradition and its five canons—invention, arrangement, style, memory, and delivery. Plato, though with mixed feelings and irony as he "wrote," condemned writing, we recall, largely as a static product that jeopardized memory, was unresponsive to its audience, and lacked the "give and take" of speech (Ong 79).

Computer-assisted writing, like that with pen and paper, addresses the first three canons. We teachers spend much time on invention. Arrangement is our structuring, and it demands appropriate layout of what students create in the invention stage. Idea processors and outliners accommodate arrangement; style analyzers (less successfully, I think) accommodate style.

Memory, too, is served by CAC and desktop publishing. Advocates believe that the computer enhances retention of information (Hocking), including, in collaborative classrooms, the comments that are made on student papers and who made them, and that its more "cognitively" readable text improves decoding, retaining, and recalling (McAfee). Further, process-oriented CAC is *discovery learning*, which, research suggests, is retained. Certainly, well-laid-out, attractive writing is easier to remember. All of us can probably recall retrieving a piece of information by visualizing it as close to a picture or a header on the left-hand side of a book.

CAC is, of course, interactive—the writer and the computer. Many have argued that *thinking* is conversation with the self and that *writing* externalizes that internal conversation. The CAC Laboratory achieves a collaborative atmosphere naturally. We hear much about the ability of the CAC teacher, an audience as well as one concerned with the student's audience, to intervene earlier in the writing process. We also hear much about the increasingly social nature of computer discourse. CAC (Plato notwithstanding) does have, to some degree, the "give and take" quality of speech.

Clearly, CAC has even more to do with presentation (the classical canon of delivery). Audience influence is felt in both directions: not only how the text influences the reader but how the reader influences the writing as the writer considers the audience prior to writing. Standard readability formulas focus on the product, not the reader. Moreover, when readability guidelines for sentence length and word frequency are applied, comprehension is not necessarily improved. Writing only 18-word sentences does not automatically equal writing *good* sentences.

Cognitive psychologists are saying that readability results from the interaction between the reader and the text and that layout and presentation are as important to comprehension as content and style. Though appreciating the linking of such features with the gestures of oral delivery, traditional writing teachers, I suspect, will not find this view very palatable. They will immediately fear, rightly, that rhetoric will be reduced to the level of decoration and will cite cases of students who have become enamored of clip art. Certainly, jobs are filled more and more often by people who can use the technology (e.g., *PageMaker*) but may know little of writing. Still, desktop publishing is another tool that can increase the persuasive power of our, and our students', writing.

A major problem cited by such leading textual writing theorists as Fred Reynolds ("Desktop Publishing and Technical Writing") is the lack of a true verbal/visual paradigm. Electronic communication has been called "secondary orality," and the phenomenon of "lateral-mindedness" (Miller) is an emergent computer "language" attempting to give to electronic writing more of the responsiveness of direct discourse. Its symbols are "emoticons" or "smileys," the latter because the punctuation at the end of the electronic-mail message is read by tilting the head to the left to see that they look like smiley faces with a colon for eyes and a hyphen for a nose.[14]

Many writing teachers do not use word processing, much less desktop publishing and the next waves of writing technology (hypertext, topographical writing, and multimedia). Composition scholars connect hypertext with reader-response theory, deconstruction, and other postmodern theories and with such current interests as writing as process, empowering the student writer, and displacing or expanding the traditional canon. Jay David Bolter, Michael Joyce, and John Smith's *Storyspace*, a hypertextual writing program, offers writers a variety of tools for creating, tracking, and editing linked texts and graphics and has been used for the teaching of writing at the Georgia Institute of Technology and Jackson Community College in Michigan. A precondition for hypertext is topical or "topographic" writing, which requires that the writer regard the text as a series of topics rather than as a continuous stream of words. Developed by "reverse engineering" from the more elaborate *Storyspace*, Bolter's *Locus* programs facilitate structured writing and writing as a process. *Locus II* permits both continuous and discrete writing; that is, borrowing the familiar analogy from quantum physics, Bolter says that the writer sometimes wants to treat his/her writing as a wave and sometimes as a particle—sometimes as a continuous flow of sentences and paragraphs and sometimes as a series of separate topics.

While *Locus I* can be used for collaboration without any special provision for networking or shared access in real time, *Locus II* offers shared real-time

---

[14]The choice of the smiley may have another reason as well, as in the "B.C." (12 July 1994) cartoon in which the Stone Age Woman goes to the beauty parlor to request "a look that has universal appeal" and comes out with a "smiley head."

access. Two or more collaborators are able to work at different locations on the same document at the same time and can coordinate their efforts both when organizing a document and when working on separate sections of a master document. Such collaboration is already possible in some word-processing environments, but, as Donald Samson (this volume) conveys so well in "Writing in High-Tech Firms," whenever several writers seated at their own computers are sharing a writing space, the result can be chaotic.

Both writing students and writers in the workplace need ready access to information. *The Interactive Notebook*, an integrated software system, is being tested at the University of Southern California. It uses hypertext to organize information serving as the basis of writing assignments and connects the students to an on-line library database to search for related sources.

Hypermedia constitute the latest wave in writing technology. We can use them to integrate writing with reading and critical thinking. In a certain sense, the Writing and Technology Curriculum Improvement Project of the Department of Community Colleges in North Carolina has set the stage. Each of the three phases culminated in a state-wide conference. The first (March, 1991) was on "Computers and the Writing Process." (I provided "An Overview of the Field of Computer-Assisted Composition.") The second (September, 1991) was on "Report Writing and Computers and Critical Thinking and Writing." Dr. John Chaffee, Director of Critical and Creative Thinking Studies at LaGuardia Community College, led a day-long seminar on the interrelationship of the writing and thinking processes. At the third (April, 1992), on "Technical Writing and Critical Thinking," Dr. Douglas Short, a consultant for IBM Multimedia Learning Technology, made a presentation on the impact of technology on reading, thinking, and writing skills and demonstrated multimedia applications for the writing classroom with *Toolbook.* He used *The Daedalus Instructional System* and *SEEN: Tutorials for Critical Reading* to show the interlinking of writing and thinking instruction. Considering writing as a visual construct clearly encompasses far more than desktop publishing.

OBSERVATION 7: INEXPERIENCE AS EDITORS

The area of greatest inexperience for the work-world writers I have dealt with is editing—of their own work and of that of others. The reason seems to be that, neither in the schools or the colleges, at least in the regular nontextual writing courses, do we have students edit. Collaborative writing classes move closer to the problem, but few, if any, English classes get into such topics as "line editing" or give students experience with editing. I asked my husband, whose doctorate is in psychology, what writing instruction he has needed that he did not receive. His quick reply was editing experience. "I'd like to be able to do to my writing what you do to it," he said. I have always read his professional work. (It has evolved, too!)

The situation is becoming more critical. Secretaries, who used to function as objective and, often, knowing readers, are becoming obsolete or finding their jobs to be very different as some CEOs and most managers write their own material directly at the computer. Similarly, writers now frequently do their own work with word processing and bypass typists, who perform editorial functions. Thus, the work of the copy editor in publishing houses increases. At the same time, one result of the publishing conglomerates has been the slashing of permanent editing positions and more reliance on free lancers. We hear that less and less editing is being done in the publishing world and can reasonably assume that the releasing of unedited or lightly edited copy into the reading world will add to our writing malaise.

If possible, I like to see writing samples prior to a workshop in order to produce generic and unidentifiable pieces for group attention. I also like to invite participants, prior to my arrival, to bring examples of their writing, particularly when they want help with a particular problem, to share with the group. Below are sample texts and phrases for discussion and "editing." I should point out that, in a real workshop, I include excellent as well as flawed samples.[15]

> **Inasmuch as writing tutoring is required for Managers on the attached list, prerequisite sessions are also open to other Managers on a voluntary basis with privilege.**

> **We were recently in contact with Medicare for any information regarding your Medicare coverage. We have also been in contact with them via telephone and FAX and we have been advised that they are unable to identify either you or your said husband as COVERED PERSONS. Therefore your assistance would be appreciated greatly at this time in supplying us with the policy effective date and your policy number under the Medicare Program. In addition to these others, we have need for a complete address for any and all of your other coverage(s) to include a street address.**

---

[15]See Carolyn Matalene's discussion (this volume) of focusing on good sentences in workshops to encourage imitation.

All Managers and General Personnel, Secretaries excluded, above Grade G-15.2 are hereby advised and put on immediate notice that they will conceptualize multiple contingency plans for whatever can, may and is likely to eventuate.

Pursuant to

As per our conversation

Per review of your files, I have concluded . . . .

Pleased be advised of the below.

The undersigned will be in touch with you again regarding . . . .

Upon receipt of the above information

Please contact the undersigned immediately upon receipt of the below information.

If the undersigned should be able to lend further clarity to the above situation . . . .

I am not free to discuss . . . .

Enclosed herewith please find . . . .

Dear Miss Logical Current Victim,

The recent theft loss that you have allegedly suffered has been referred to the below signatory for handling. Enclosed please find a complete set of our Personal (etc.) Property Inventory Forms which are to be used in detailing your apparent losses. Please complete all of the information columns, # 1-21, and return to the signatory below for processing. Processing time will be related, it is to be appreciated, to the accuracy and thoroughness with which you respond to this request by the signatory below.

Pursuant to the conditions of the policy granted to you by this company it is necessary for you to provide documentation for every item that you intend to claim against your policy with this company.   Said documentation normally consist of receipts from the original purchase of said items, canceled checks, the records from charge accounts, instruction manuals, ownership manuals, warranties sheets, invoices for repairs to said items, and photographs.   In the unfortunate circumstance that you are unable to provide documentation of this type, please forward to the below signatory other information that can be accepted as reasonable proof of ownership.   NOTE: The respondent is cautioned to provide ORIGINALS of all proofs of ownership.   Photocopies will not be accepted as proof of ownership.

Upon receipt of the above information by the below signatory, the handling of your claim can be preceeded with.   In the event that any questions remain have no hesitation to call the below signatory at the telephone number above.   Assistance is a hallmark of our company.

Sincerely,

An alternative approach, if the technology is available, is to have pairs of participants work together at computers (*pairs* to emphasize and to practice collaboration on the small as well as the large scale). Each screen has the samples available to edit and change as writing duos deem appropriate. The writing trainer sits at his/her own computer, making (copying) the changes from each pair. Ultimately, the composite sample is projected on a large screen for discussion by the group.

Another simple and invaluable approach is using the computer's "word count" tool. Much of the writing I do is limited to 2,000 or 2,500 or some precise number of words. I have learned much about my own writing by being forced to "edit" it for such maximums. I usually have to give workshop participants a "canned" draft to "downsize" at their computers, but I prefer, as in the English class, to have the students write a longer theme and then reduce it to, say, 1,500 words.

OBSERVATION 8: THE (LOGICAL) EMOTIONAL NEED FOR "SEIZE-ONs"

Teaching writing workshops to adults requires, much more than teaching students, moving from "seize-the-day" thinking, in which they are generally adept, to "seize the way." Their world is hurried; the workshop itself is likely to be robbing them of "time on the floor"; they are impatient because "all this" should have been given to them in school and in such a way that they could grasp it; they are professionals who *know* their fields; and they are suspicious of claims that the field of English or writing can't be "known" in the same way and is, in fact, quite wishy-washy. They want and need something concrete to take away from the session(s). They are too street-smart to be easily fooled by the cutesy/glitzy/sound-bitey masquerading as the substantive.

Under "Observation 3: Writing Baggage: Love–Hate Memories of Teachers," I, implicitly at least, indicated that I begin by admitting that language constantly changes and that today's poor speakers and writers can be forgiven when we recognize that their errors have precedents. I mean my audience to infer the need for tolerance—of others and of themselves and not with regard only to English. I mean to be as honest as I can about the imprecision of my profession and about what I try to do in the face of that imprecision. I mean to give them *Seize-Ons.* (I am careful to point out that the *bona fides* of these Seize-Ons are only that they have worked for me.) I mean to embed these in context that is likely to be remembered long after "bare rules" will have disappeared or become garbled. I also distinguish *Macro* and *Micro Seize-Ons* (where others speak of, for example, "higher order" and "lower order" concerns). The following are a few examples. They vary, of course, from group to group because the audience affects what I say and how I say it. I am adept at reading from a written text without appearing to read and like to have a written text (always), but I may well "ad lib" much of what is on the page, particularly if the group is very upbeat, enthusiastic, and "with me."

A—EXAMPLES OF MACRO "SEIZE-ONs"

Sample Macro "Seize-On" 1—*Be* the Writer.

What happens when you write is largely inexplicable, a mix of you, your experiences (past and this morning), the topic or task that confronts you, your sense of your audience .... The process that ensues yields a product that is synergistic. Take up your pen/pencil or open a file on your computer. Sit poised for no more than thirty seconds and then write—something, anything. *Be* the writer. A truism of Psychology is that attitude follows behavior. Act the writer and become the writer.

Sample Macro "Seize-On" 2—Imprint and Prepare for the White Rabbit and for Taking It on the *Neck*.

When I was a fledgling English professor, I provided topics for writing assignments (though always including the option of "A Topic of Your Own Choosing"). I urged students not to let the topic dictate to them, however, but to make it their own and use it as a springboard for their creativity, altering it as necessary.[16] Some years later, a student cited this common sense as the most important learning she did in my class and *as a guideline for all the areas of her life*. I was embarrassed (and pleased, of course). I was fumbling toward the marriage of structure and creativity.

Excluding yourself from or obscuring yourself in the writing you must perform cheats you, the writing, and the audience/readers, including your collaborators (those above you in the hierarchy, anyone who reads and comments on your work, any co-authors). Obviously, if you work in a government agency where the "byline" is at best a committee, the earlier you write in the process, the more "you" will appear. Yet, though the individual tends to be diluted as the cycles of reading and response widen and repeat, the challenge stands tall: Did "your" idea survive? Did it trigger thoughts in other writers? Is it better than when you launched it? Did your favorite phrasing please others?

I am not being subversive of organizational culture. I recognize that your most interesting comments are likely to be controversial and that you write in political times and places. I don't expect corporate writers to be individualistic in the way of Hemingway (though novelist Kurt Vonnegut was trained at General Electric). Yet, next to speaking, writing remains our most basic form of communication. As writers, we must communicate to our audiences and, even in the workplace, perhaps especially in the workplace, retain the right to be an individual (to provide a touch of personality, humor, distinctiveness).

Americans will not again tolerate assembly-line work conditions and certainly not in a creative field like writing. Writing, again, is a mix of you, your experiences (past and this morning), the topic or task that confronts you, your sense of your audience . . . . Now we add to the mix the input of others. In today's world, no country, much less an individual, can remain isolated and survive. What you do in your on-the-job writing is, in effect, a model for larger and larger arenas.

Work writing is often team writing, but, if only one writer is involved, the writing is still not purely individualistic, involving, as we have seen, so many elements, some of them unconscious, that "work together." Such recent workplace movements as Quality Circles and Total Quality both bless and damn the individual. While, in education, faculty remain skeptical of TQM as a fad, the chief fear I hear among staff is the loss of individuality[17] —"Will we have 'Group of the Month' instead of 'Employee of the Month'?" As a writer and a person, you must find that *creative tension* between being an individual and being part of a team—ultimately between being an individual, being a member of a group (the middle class, Hispanics, managers . . .), and being a member of the larger

---

[16]See Hunter: "After the semester is underway, topic invention becomes a strong emphasis [in Hunter's creative writing course]. The idea is to blend the creative process into the writing of required papers by finding topics which deal with personal material. As skill in finding topics (about which they are genuinely interested) develops, many students realize they do not, as they had previously believed, 'hate writing.' They begin to like to write clearly and see the point of mastering grammar and mechanics."

[17]If I have time or find the participants amenable, I point out that Terry Mollner (*The Relationship Age*) and the Trusteeship Institute, Inc., have adapted the Mondragon model of Spain to allow for the North American cultural bent of individuality. Applied at Nelco Mechanical Ltd., a construction company in Kitchener, Ontario, this "Trusteeship Cooperative" permits volunteers to join while other employees remain as they are, with the option of becoming members at the first of any month.

culture (America, the world . . .).

Einstein put it this way: "What the individual can do is give a fine example, and have the courage to firmly uphold [sic for the split infinitive!] ethical convictions in a society of cynics" (wallboard, Museum of Science and Energy, Oak Ridge, Tennessee). In the writing context, you may think, initially, of those who "edit" (read and comment on) your work as the "cynics." If you have to conclude that they are on power trips or are writing something because they must to prove they have completed their job, offset them by extracting and applying every smidgen of usefulness from their comments. How much better, however, to be able to think of them positively, indeed, of their being able to comment on your work because it has "sent them higher" in the first place.

Early in my career, I stumbled on a simple technique that has helped me with academic publishing. When an editor returned an article to me, I would scan any comments of readers to see if I had missed a typo or made a grammatical booboo. I would make any such changes and have the article in the mail again that same day or ready for the next day's mail. I confess that I have seldom spent much time on what the readers meant as more substantive criticism.

In the days before writing and printing, when we were "oralists" perforce, our bards and poets functioned partly by the use of "formulas." Their works were highly "formulaic" but simultaneously individualistic and creative. Today's high tech world of boilerplate and your own world of personal macros that you have developed to save time with your regular writing projects, then, have, strangely, an affinity with that long-gone past. Modern jazz functions in much the same way: the musician is always prepared but leaves room for the unexpected, indeed anticipates the unexpected both in "reaching the groove" and "in the groove."

I hope many of us reach times when, for one little moment, we can do no wrong. The project comes together, the teaching hits the mark, the audience is with us, the writing is brilliant, and . . . . When I find that moment, I feel it as chills up and down the back of my neck. Taking it on my neck like that makes up for all the times I "take it on the chin" from others. I call it the Pym Syndrome. Barbara Pym was a British novelist who wrote mostly about old maids and small lives at the tea cup, but she has a character who *imagines suddenly having a white rabbit thrust into her arms.* I believe that writers and people in general have the right to expect experiences comparable to that—always possibility, always looking forward to the next whatever. Think about writing as preparing for your next white rabbit, for those "thrills" of the neck. Think about coming to work every day as preparing for your next white rabbit . . . . Remember, too: "If you build it, they will come" (*Field of Dreams*).

Time permitting, I cite other examples. At the least, I like to provide a handout of "authenticating" quotations for the participants to take away and think about. Generally, they have never "come at" writing from such levels/concerns before. I keep a computer bank of these to which I am constantly adding. A standby for creativity within rules is Bill Russell: "My problem is that I'm constantly running into people who expect me to do things that offend me and my sense of freedom, so I've spent a lot of time trying to establish a set of principles that will both protect my freedom and respect theirs" (*Second Wind* 193). Here's a wonderful one on the relationship between creativity and *any* kind of writing from an article that is forthcoming in one of the journals I edit:

. . . . ANY kind of good writing, is, or ought to be, creative. I believe good writing happens when the writer learns to access and express her/his genuine concerns. In my experience as a writer, this accessing-and-expressing is the core, center, root—the foundation and prime mover—of any composing process.

How does this theory translate into practice? It's a clumsy, unpredictable, wild, and funny dance, like the ballet of Disney's hippos. I don't know how to turn the English Composition curriculum into a ballerina, but I can put it in a tutu and teach it to listen to Swan Lake.

. . .

. . . the creative mind can be engaged even when writing research, analysis, or an essay test. . . . (Hunter)

In future workshops, I will assuredly refer to Joyce Magnotto's pointing out, in "Writing in a Bureaucracy" (this volume), that auditors in the Department of Labor describe their writing as "formulaic" or "boilerplate"!

Sample Macro "Seize-On" 3—Know Your Audience and View Your Audience as Your Customer.

Know your audience. The question about who will read (or hear) your presentation should be near the top of your checklist for writing.[18] Must you be formal or informal? Do your readers know your topic, or are they reading to find out about it? Are you writing for, as categories, business people, children, or average adults? If you were the audience/reader for this particular topic, what would you want and need to know, and "how" would you want to learn it? What makes you feel "patronized"?

Let me pause here to commit heresy. Someone in your company will probably run the Gunning Fog Index or the Flesch Scale or some readability instrument on your writing. Its level will likely be assessed as "too high." Analyze why. As the writer, you are obligated to be clear. If your writing is clear but for words that are "too hard" or that introduce new concepts . . ., stand up for it (gently and reasonably). We have discussed ways of explaining-without-seeming-to-explain in this workshop. We have talked, at least briefly, about the obligations of readers. Until writers like you take a stand against Dumbing Down, we will keep on dumbing

---

[18]Most companies and groups have an in-house checklist for writers in their style manuals. (Joyce Magnotto includes one from the General Accounting Office in her chapter. Carolyn Matalene cites that of the National Conference of Commissioners on Uniform State Laws.) If they do not, I work with the participants to "build" one. We generally address audience, topic, purpose, style, opening, standard (and standing) information, points to be made in this document, methods of highlighting the points, and exit.

down. (I can't imagine the ultimate in dumbing down!) **Besides, many readers in Readerland appreciate learning something from what they read.**

Whether the members of your writing audience are internal (your supervisor, co-workers, the Board) or external (the "real," literal consumers of your company's products or services), you might find the application of a Total Quality technique useful: think of all of your audiences as "customers" who purchase your product voluntarily.

The composition classroom is an artificial construct. English professors will not be one's audience in the after-life of college (except in the few instances in which people become college professors), and we English teachers probably do not spend enough of our precious teaching time on this topic.[19]

Some of the disagreements about writing discussed in "Observation 5: The Great Writing Divide: 'Lofty Professor' Versus 'Friendly Neighbor' Writing," particularly those within Academia and its offspring, relate to audience. I want us, as teachers, to talk with students about their roles as writers and as readers and about curbing and curing the disease of Dumbing Down. One of the best literary figures to use toward such ends is Reynolds Price. He writes for more "different" audiences than anyone I know, but he makes every reader, I suspect, feel that he/she is an intelligent human being.

Writing requires a union of writer and audience. (*Diagrammatic Writing Using Word Processing* [Sadler, Greene, and Sadler] asks the author to identify his or her audience for each rhetorical mode.) Good topics, good writing, good literature (and good people) pull us forward. The writer is accountable for clarity, assuredly, but also for enriching the reader in some way, for *teaching* something—content, style, a single new word, a different point of view—*something*. Writerhood must meet such obligations. Readerhood must acknowledge and demand them. Readers are at least as important to writers as writers to readers. Even young writers must focus on audience as natural to the writing process.

If we can get into the heads and hearts of young writers the synergism of structure and creativity, writer and subject matter, and writer and reader and if we can get all of us to reach up rather than down, we will solve

---

[19]Shifting back and forth among audiences for this chapter, as I played writer to you, my reader, and writing trainer in the workplace workshop or identified with writing teachers or workshop participants and students, was interesting. Occasionally, I would forget and write "to-my-participants" material in the form of chapter text. Visual aids (e.g., the boxes) were crucial and again underscored for me the complexity of writing and the overlapping of its ingredients. I was particularly bemused when, looking for a different way to highlight, I broke out my imagined "prescriptions" of an in-house writing specialist yielding to Dumbing Down with the medical-pharmaceutical symbol. It also suggested "prescriptive writing" for me.

more than our problems with writing. Expectation is also still key. If the teacher/individual acts as though he/she expects high performance from students/other individuals (no matter their social level), much will come. When we mingle all these threads, we are doing Big Writing. The term derives from an insult. One of the saddest pieces of correspondence I received as a college president was the anonymous letter from a student berating me for quoting Milton (and others) and for Big Writing. With the latter, he meant to deliver the unkindest cut of all. I wish I could always be guilty as charged. Big Writing is not just the stuff of anecdote; it is an antidote for our writing (and reading) ills.

I think that young writers will like Big Writing. They can run around singing—

> I wish I may,
> I wish I might,
> Do BIG WRITING
> With all my might!

(The last line could have been "Even at night" to get at the unconscious thought processes of good writing, but children like word play, too, and teachers can have them ponder *might* and *might*.) They (and we) might even be doing "big living" at the same time.

Sample Macro "Seize-On" 4—Know Your "Rhetorical Mode" of Writing.

If nothing else has convinced you of my off-the-wall-ness, Macro "Seize-On" 4 may. Why would you, all grown up and in the workplace, ever possibly need one of those "rhetorical modes" or "types" of writing you were taught or should have been taught in high school and/or college? Well, when you are given a writing task, would the following questions help you decide how to approach it?

1   Do you want to describe x number of aspects of the subject?

2   Do you want to tell a story about the subject? [Not so remote— what if you're writing the history of your company or of a product?]

3   Do you want to explain that the subject is a perfect example of _____ ?

4   Do you want to define the subject or some aspect of it?

5   Do you want to compare and contrast the subject with something else?

6   Do you want to write about the procedure(s) involved in the subject?

7   Do you want to divide the subject into groups or types?

8   Do you want to explain how the subject causes/has caused certain events to occur?

9   Do you want to prove something about the subject?

These questions, in turn, transform, presto change-o, into the nine basic types or modes of discourse:

1	**Description**
2	**Narration**
3	**Example**
4	**Definition**
5	**Comparison/Contrast**
6	**Process**
7	**Classification**
8	**Cause and Effect**
9	**Argument**

Any writing that you do in the workplace is likely to be a variation on one of these basic types or to combine several of the types.

During the workshop, we zoom in on the types that the participants are most curious about (often because they seem at farthest remove from writing in their workplace) or find most applicable.

We need to focus more in school and college English on the modes of discourse. Last year, for the first time, North Carolina administered a writing test to its own fourth graders. The state average for students demonstrating "proficiency" was 24%. They had 50 minutes to complete the following assignment: "Think about a special day that you have had. Tell about what happened that was special."

Older students have been taking a writing test for some time. It alternates "explanation" and "description," and they tend to perform better on the "explanatory" writing. As with the fourth graders, their task is implicit; they are not directed to employ a specific genre, type, or rhetorical mode but must infer what is required.

A standard response to such dismal reports is that teachers must require more writing. All of us surely agree, but students must also know about and aim for Big Writing. Additional "uninformed" writing will make them more facile writers—but of generally uninformed writing. If they are to be tested on description, narration, example, definition, comparison/contrast, process, classification, cause and effect, or argumentation, they must, at the least, know the demands of each mode. To be Big Writers, they must know more. Although narrative was required by this recent test, all good writing—narrative most of all—lives in a tension between structure and creativity and in the interplay of author and audience.

Further, the graded samples of the fourth-grade writing provided by the State Department of Public Instruction reveal as much about class/economic differences as level of preparation. The "better" student tells about being taken to an animal shelter to choose a dog:

> Mom said that I could name the dog. I looked at the white dog for a long time. He reminded me of a golf ball, which reminded me of bogies. So I decided to name him Bogey. it [sic] was the perfect name.

Here is the sum of the "poor" specimen:

> My special day was my birthday. I had alot of friends come over. We played games and watched T.V. Then we had cake and ice cream. After that we oped my preast. Then we went inside and played Nintendo. We had a good time. We also got to stay up to 12:30. I had a sleep over. I will say we had a very good time.

The label is ironically apt; its "poorer" author probably is unfamiliar with animal shelters and golf. We can also infer a bit about the influence of technology from the contrast in spelling within it: "oped" and "preast" on the one hand and "Nintendo" on the other. (Technology will always be only as good as its user. It does not replace the requirement *to learn* in "learner.") "Alot" knows no class boundaries.

Teachers alone cannot solve the social problem. They *can* teach the different modes of writing, urge independence and creativity in plying them, and get students to respond to the higher call of "big writing."

One of the motivations for producing Sadler, Greene, and Sadler's *Diagrammatic Writing Using Word Processing,* the CAC program from which I principally draw the material on rhetorical modes that I use in writing workshops, was the report that so many students failed the North Carolina Competency Examination because they did not understand the *kind* of writing they were asked to produce. Its tutorials were developed largely from Dr. Wendy Greene's one-on-one sessions with adult students and from techniques in her (and my) regular English classes. They are not computer-bound. A subsection of "Pre-Writing" called "Establishing the Approach" asks a series of questions to identify the mode in which the writer wants to work. For example, "Narrative" is chosen by answering "yes" to the question, "Do you want to *tell a story about* [the subject]?" That genre is identified and, in the "Writing" section, the writer chooses it from among the nine traditional expository modes. After reading the sample narrative essay, he/she proceeds to the "Tutorial" in that mode and is quizzed on what is learned about narration. In the last section, "Building Bones," the writer builds the skeleton of the essay itself, gradually producing the most important sentences in the composition: the thesis, topic sentences for each body paragraph and for the concluding paragraph, a "grabber" (the first sentence of the essay) and a "zinger" (the last). The program keeps each major piece of the text being constructed in front of the writer as the next piece is being worked on to preserve the "larger vision" of the writing-in-process.

Teachers can use a kindred approach without computers (though I advocate them as a writing tool promoting both process and product). Young children respond well to rote (to "wrote" if teachers have their way!). Jingles about what the writer must do to create narrative (or any other rhetorical mode) can become entirely natural, can be made part of the knee jerks of childhood/writerhood/writingclasshood. Such basic formulaic approaches can form the backbone for more and more advanced writing. By the time the fourth graders take their test, they will know the ingredients of narration (or description or argumentation or . . .).

Students continue to have trouble performing the *kind* of writing being requested. What if the test writers added to the assignment, "Think about a special day that you have had. Tell about what happened that was special," this short second paragraph?

> We are asking you to write a *narrative*. Remember that *narration* involves [the several components that the students have recited and practiced since the *first* grade]. As always, however, do not let the "rules" limit you. They are the skeleton of your writing, but you put the meat on these bones. Add yourself to your writing. Give your reader lively details!

B—EXAMPLES OF MICRO "SEIZE-ONs"

I find hard-down grammar errors such as "he seen," "irregardless," and double negatives ("can't hardly") relatively rare in *adult* writing populations. Rather, at the micro level, they need more "sophisticated" tutoring, particularly if the participants in the workshop are managers. Let me offer one example for the kind of "embedding" I like to do.

Micro "Seize-On"—The Split Infinitive

My husband never lies to me. If he does lie to me, the lie comes true.

As much as I liked *Star Trek*, I detested its prologue with "to boldly go where no man has ever gone before"—mainly for the split infinitive ("to boldly go") but, to a lesser extent, for the *man* bit. My husband wanted me to watch it with him. "Why," he said, "William Shatner is a Shakespearean actor! Would you miss watching a Shakespearean actor?"

We later discovered that Shatner had acted at Stratford—in Canada!

I go on, of course, to claim split infinitives as one of *my* "hang-ups"; to indicate that they are actually a problem in Latin rather than English; to quote Winston Churchill; to indicate that I would always let my English students split them if they wrote me a marginal note stating that they knew they were doing so and meant to do so; and to warn this audience, nonetheless, that the "finicky" will turn up their noses if they split them.

A LIST OF OTHER SAMPLE MICRO "SEIZE-ONs"

Here is a typical list of other Micro "Seize-Ons" that I may work through with groups when I have not had the opportunity to review samples of their "real" in-house writing and draw from it:

among/between
"and etc."
"between you and I," "to you and I," etc.
can/may
compare to/with
continually/continuously
"could of," "might of"
"different than"
each other/one another
"enthuse"
"ever since"
fewer/less
"fillers"—there (is, are, were), it (is, was, has been)
"firstly," "secondly," "thirdly"
"fix"
flammable/inflammable
former/latter
graduate (verb) vs. *graduate* (noun)
hanged/hung
hopefully
imply/infer
"is when," "is where"
-*ize*—"aromatize," "chauffeurize," "accessorize," "historize," "youthfulize," "bracketize,"
"competitorize"
lend/loan
media—plural
modification of *unique*
"more importantly" (for *more important*)
"orientate" for *orient*
passive voice: when to use (when you don't know the "doer" or need to protect his/her identity,
when the doer is not important) and when not to use
phenomenon/phenomena
raise/rear
"The reason is because . . . ."
that vs. *which* to introduce clauses
thing
type as an adjective
-*wise*—"budgetwise," "departmentwise," "companywise," "efficiencywise" (Language-wise,
she's simply incorrect.)

"Discovery learning" is effective at every level, and I like to start the examples with an overhead and let the participants add to them from their own experiences. Again, computers enhance the exercise by letting them "write" (publicly) as well as discuss. Below are samples:

MALAPROPS

I saw four polo bears in the Galapagos Islands recently.

As a result of that one small victory, he was immediately capitulated into media prominence.

I assume you concur that she is a person of integrity and moral turpitude.

PUNCTUATION

comma before *because*

colon before *are, is*

REDUNDANCIES

*young juveniles
past history
a real lifelike actuality of today
*free gifts
*unnecessary waste
old standby
*successfully predicted
*No trespassing without permission.

Note: The terms marked with asterisks appear in Edwin Newman's
Strictly Speaking.

ANTILOGIES

student teacher

pretty ugly

SPELLING

"alot"

TODAY'S "Buzz Word"—DAY-AFTER-TOMORROW'S "Cliché"

ball park figure

bottom line

cutting edge

multifaceted

real challenges

red-letter day

selling like hot cakes

EXAMPLES OF "JIT LISTS"

I always end the "micro" session(s) by encouraging the workshop participants to construct private and personal "Just In Time" (JIT) sheets or cards,
preferably billfold-sized. JIT is a Total Quality concept drawn from the
Japanese *kanban* system, and it has altered the inventory control procedures of American business. Vast amounts of goods are no longer stored in
expensive-to-maintain warehouses but are on-site when needed ("just in
time"). The fact that JIT is *process-* rather than *outcome-/product-driven*
also makes it compatible with writing. I can never remember some of
the "microtia" of English (and other areas), and I want access at the moment of need (i.e., "just in time"). Here are several personal JIT Lists that I
share[20]:

---

[20]I also point out that I use JIT Lists in other arenas, for example, for computer figures,
such as the cedilla and the degrees sign, which are not on the keyboard; Roman numerals
from fifty up; autographing protocol: *for* if the person is buying the book, *to* if the author is
giving it; formulas for sonnets, ballads, and other poetic forms; instructions (how to do
double-sided printing on our copier as opposed to our laser printer; how to construct fractions
on the computer).

JIT List 1—Comparison

Compare to—when the items are regarded as similar

Compare with—when both similarities and differences are to
be considered

JIT List 2—Time References

biannual—twice each year

biennial—happening every second year, lasting two years; an event that occurs every
two years

bimonthly—every two months

biweekly—once in two weeks

biyearly—once in two years

perennial—lasting/active through one year or many years; perpetual

quadrennially—every four years; quadrennial—happening once in four years; lasting for
four years

semimonthly—twice a month

semiweekly—twice a week

semiyearly—twice a year

triennially—every three years; triennial—occurring every third year, lasting three
years; a third anniversary

JIT List 3—Spelling

any more

anyhow

anyway

awhile

every time

everyday (adjective)

full-time

JIT List 4—Ensure vs. Insure

Ensure—implies a making certain, inevitable

Insure—stresses the taking of necessary measures beforehand to make a result certain or provide for any probable contingency

(Note: Insure that you just use *insure*!)

JIT List 5—Shall and Will

I—Futurity

First Person—shall

Second Person—will

Third Person—will

II—Determination

First Person—will

Second Person—shall

Third Person—shall

Note: This usage is an Anglicism; ignore it except in the most formal, scholarly contexts.

IMPLICATIONS FOR THE CURRICULUM

I'm in my English classroom, and, just prior to a polite knock on its door, the back of my neck begins to sing. Sure enough, when I respond, it's the white rabbit: I'm to have my way with English Composition.

Presto change-o. I've increased the standard 3-hour freshman writing class to 6 hours, patterning it after the science laboratory course, with 4 hours of credit for 3 hours of lecture-discussion and a 3-hour computer laboratory.[21]

The class has modules (components) demonstrating, dialoguing about, and practicing every major classification of writing (e.g., belles-lettres, creative, expository, textual), as well as reading samples of each. Literature, if only via the references I bring in, as the following excerpt from Pope's *An Essay on Criticism* for "form as meaning" and "learned skills," will buttress the course throughout; I don't ever want to divorce literature from composition.

> True ease in writing comes from art, not chance,
> As those move easiest who have learn'd to dance.
> 'Tis not enough no harshness gives offence,
> The sound must seem an Echo to the sense:
> Soft is the strain when Zephyr gently blows,
> And the smooth stream in smoother numbers flows;
> But when loud surges lash the sounding shore,
> The hoarse, rough verse should like the torrent roar:
> When Ajax strives some rock's vast weight to throw,
> The line too labours, and the words move slow;
> Not so, when swift Camilla scours the plain,
> Flies o'er th' unbending corn, and skims along the main. (11. 62–73)

One module is devoted to editing, and, in addition to learning to edit at different levels, we read poetry, trying to grasp and apply its pithiness and its techniques of form as meaning as we edit our own prose into more concise form. Students are self-editors and colleague editors throughout. They also write collaboratively, and at least one exercise is a communal writing project under simulated deadline conditions.

In fact, we will simulate writing conditions, as appropriate, for each component, using the CAC Laboratory to practice what we have heard and talked about in class. I will bring in (or take us to) workplace writers and trainers, who describe what they do and what they need for their writing.

I do all of the assignments and go to the CAC Laboratory with my students. I keep a private log of observations about what happens during their exchanges here and in the classroom.

---

[21]Dr. Wendy Tibbetts Greene and I have been running around the country for years promoting this one, with, so far as we know, zero success.

The course begins by placing writing in the larger context of the human condition and probing the truth of the view that we are what we write (say) and of the assertion of "effective use of the English language as the most reliable safety net life has to offer." To insure that I don't get too soapboxy as we ponder communication, I advise the students to read some of Franz Kafka's works—for example, *The Penal Colony*—and watch tapes of the movies *Cool Hand Luke* (Strother Martin's "What we have here is a failure to communicate") and *The Jayhawkers* (Fess Parker's "grammar" lesson for two French children). This is but the first of many occasions upon which I will reference movies. (I love movies!)

We dialogue about writing, its importance, its relation to being human, its complexity, and why people fear writing and make mistakes on which we pounce. We sample historical precedents for some of those mistakes, setting the stage for the inference of tolerance. We spend some time discussing the two conflicting skills required in writing—creating and editing—and ways of improving their marriage. We talk about the skills required to write, about improving those skills, and about the *je ne sais quoi* that is beyond skills. We try to be honest about the definitiveness of writing (the great body of theory that now supports it) or the lack thereof (the variations in its conventions). We speak of writers as *professionals*, of what that implies about writers and about ourselves as we try on that terminology, view ourselves and other writers as professionals, and engage in *being* writers, a pledge we make for the duration of this class and ever after. We explore why that stance is important, particularly in the days of Dumbing Down. We think upon the obligations of writers and the obligations of readers; we think upon Big Writing. We agree not to play the game of "Lofty Professor" Versus "Friendly Neighbor" Writing and not to subvert any of the kinds of writing in our modules but, rather, to seek the commonalities that contain them all, including creativity and individualism. We talk of the historical development of communication, including the Age of Rhetoric, Plato's objections to writing, apologia (notably in the Renaissance) for writing, the changes brought by technology and theories that it is reachieving the classical canons. We sample, discuss, and practice the nine basic rhetorical modes and assess how they buttress and support every kind of writing that we will be doing. We take the simple matter of writing as a visual construct (organized, "broken out," say something/show something prose) and find that it is far from simple. In fact, it takes us to explorations of CAC, desktop publishing, hypertext, topographical writing, multimedia. . . . A student in my class who is the reigning campus wizard of emoticons agrees to demonstrate them when we talk about our search for "a true verbal/visual paradigm."

I may not be able to do justice to all of these. Collaboration is a principal technique of the class. My department and colleagues model it. All of us are pleased to be covering the same topics in the composition course. One

of our technical writing specialists, the head of the School of Business, and
other colleagues visit all of the classes or, as a change of pace, do presentations for our combined students. I get to talk about CAC. We have a
Computer Demonstration Laboratory at our college, and its director demon-
strates hypertext, multimedia, . . . and helps students complete their research
assignment via Internet or CompuServe. Several adult students agree to talk
about writing in their workplaces.

As we teachers are teaching, we have opportunities to expand our knowledge base. Staff (e.g., the head of the CAC Laboratory) and faculty (e.g., a
composition theorist) offer regular presentations on the basics and on developments in their respective fields. A member of the Department of Psychology tells us about "cognitive readability," and I work with him/her to
adapt its techniques to the class-in-progress and to future classes. The students get off onto reader/audience and writer linkage after that presentation,
and I ask the psychologist[22] back to help us. (I am always mindful that this
is a class-in-progress and that it can model what it teaches, in this instance,
the influence of participants and audience.) I'm also working on developing
courses in "Teaching Writing" for my colleagues (and the World!) and for
student teachers. (I am anticipating and preparing for more visits from more
white rabbits. So are the students—for ever after and forever after.)

If my college is small, I cajole my department chair, dean, and/or president
into under*writing* (pun intended!) visiting scholars (among them, Joyce Magnotto, Carolyn Matalene, Fred Reynolds, and Don Samson!) or my own
research/presentation of research in one of these fields. One hook I use is
this new Total Quality muck. I may not believe it relates to writing, but who
knows? (I do; I will set forth for the students at least 15 minutes' worth of
Total Quality and its application to writing, their own JIT Lists included.
Yes, I admit that I will give 15 minutes also to collaboration—all the way
out to Valuing Differences.) Besides, Total Quality is guaranteed to get the
president's interest and get us looked at, for the first time ever, through
rose-colored glasses.

. . .

Clichés are "bad," we know, unless we can "make *hey*" with them. What
a way to revolutionize the "rabbit test"!

---

[22]I am also working with him/her on finding teaching strategies to enact learning styles
and developing software to help students discern and maximize their individual learning styles.

APPENDIX A: Teachers Remembered

To: Teacher Appreciation Week
The Sanford Herald
P.O. Box 100
Sanford, North Carolina 27331-0100

From: Lynn Veach Sadler

Date: May 2, 1994

Thank you for the opportunity!

Word Count: 199 words (material below)

I don't pronounce the *l* in "salmon" or melt "ice cream" with a long Southern *i* because Miss Mary Lou Wilkins, my ninth-grade English teacher (Warsaw), helped me not to. More important, she taught me the *way* to correct: without embarrassing, without slaying the spirit. Her complimenting a fellow student for describing a De Maupassant character's hands influenced my writing. Elegant and bejeweled, she tripped daily from the Southern "bandbox." No one ever whispered old maid stereotypes about *her*.

Bert Smith (now retired outside Sanford) taught me high school chemistry. If I was his "pet," as I tended to be for most teachers, he gave no indication—to me or anyone else, though I would occasionally think I saw his eyes sparkle when I answered a question. Like Miss Wilkins, he was very professional, but he helped, after school, every student who would let him help and magnetized students who eschewed help.

"Bert" drove to Vermont for my inauguration as a college president. Miss Wilkins, who was blind then and has since died, sent a home-made pound cake for the private dinner I had invited her to at the President's home. Great teachers pervade.

Lynn Veach Sadler

APPENDIX B:
Excerpt from Lynn Veach Sadler, "Total Quality Management: The Issues of Change," TQM and Education: A Conference for the Community College System of North Carolina, Southwestern Community College, Sylva, North Carolina, April 19–20, 1993

Making Business Palatable to the Academic World

Someone also has to make "business" palatable to the academic world. As others have pointed out and all of us know, academicians, aside from those who interact with business (many in the community college) or are in the School of Business, are skeptical about stereotypical figure-slinging bottom-liners. We need to share with them some of the "relevant trivia" of industry: Branch Rickey, in the "business" of baseball, hiring Jackie Robinson in 1947; novelist Kurt Vonnegut being trained at General Electric; H. J. Heinz running a worldwide poetry contest for its employees and commissioning some of the world's best artists to illustrate the ten winning entries and printing them in its annual report (1982).

We consider corporate training programs and corporate colleges as poachers on our territory, but we also need to think about the implications of many of the most successful industries speaking of themselves in and being thought of in "our" terms. For example, we hear frequent references to "Levi Strauss University." CRS Sirrine was started to design schools and has created many colleges/universities; working there is likened to being a graduate student. Armstrong Manor, where new hires receive three months of training and orientation, is like a dormitory, actually apparently more like the "residence hall" of contemporary academic parlance. Bell Laboratories is supposedly the closest approximation to the academic to be found in a commercial environment. Its Murray Hill complex is said to look like a college campus. Interesting questions about North Carolina's Research Triangle Park come to mind. Fisher-Price's on-site nursery school is both laboratory and employee benefit in the same vein as the day care center maintained by a college. Control Data, through *PLATO*, claims to be second only to the Department of Defense in training Americans (elementary through college students, non-students, its own employees). We also need to remember the success of our so-called "entrepreneurial" academic institutions and the fact that real entrepreneurs, in business and everywhere, plan for the future by *taking advantage of* the past.

If academics in general think of business at all, they simply tacitly nod when their administrators (the members of the President's Cabinet but usually the President) pontificate about industry providing internships for "our" students, jobs for "our" graduates, and monetary support. We have to stop looking to business only for such ends and focus on its new, ultimately "moral" ways. Remember the letter from the AT&T manager in New Jersey: "holistic ethical and self-improvement approaches" (see Appendix C). Academicians need to know that business is doing more than just the school and college partnerships that can be seen as in its best interests.[23] Atlantic Richfield is committed to improving the public education system. Cummins Engine has long insisted that business has *social* as well as economic responsibilities. The Erie Insurance Building at Perry Square reclaimed its neighborhood from urban blight, and its cafeteria is probably the largest facility in America operated by the legally blind. (On the campus, we fret about the costs of accommodating handicapped students.) H. B. Fuller Company is environmentally concerned, and its St. Paul headquarters is becoming a nature preserve. In contrast, when the students at the University of North Carolina at Chapel Hill celebrate victories, notably the NCAA Tournament, nature is more likely to be decimated. (My own undergraduate institution, Duke, is probably just as bad; Chapel Hill gets more publicity.) H. B. Fuller also nurtures the volunteer activities of its employees and has a Rape and Sexual Assault Legal Advocate Program in Minneapolis. Levi Strauss, which caters to our students, is another "socially responsible" company. Known not only for fairness to women, minorities, and the handicapped, it has a unique "Social Benefits Program" to encourage employees to be active in educational and community activities. A criterion for Rhodes Scholars is concern for their fellow humans. How many of us can claim "socially responsible" campuses? At your leisure, look in the handouts at the *operating principles, values, beliefs, thoughts (will's), way, cornerstones, tenets, foundations, credo*, or what have you—even the choice of vocabulary is interesting and significant—of Apple, Armstrong, Celestial Seasonings, Dana, Hewlett-Packard, IBM, Kollmorgen, Marion Laboratories, and W. L. Gore & Associates. They sound like academic mission statements, but the best companies make them pervasive.

Woodrow Wilson, in his inauguration address as the President of Princeton, told the student body that social service was the highest law of duty; the educated person, he believed, must not sit still and know but do and act. Yet, we do little more on our campuses than pay lip service, if that, to the moral. (Wilson also said, by the way, that, compared with the college politician, the real article seemed like an amateur.) Do even our best colleges *live* their mission statements?

At least a few businesses have modeled "valuing differences" (which I think has to be part of Total Quality), their version of supporting cultural diversity, though on largely pragmatic grounds: preparation for the work-

---

[23]We are always suspicious, e.g., the critics of Eli Lilly's sponsorship of advertisements urging the depressed to get help (its antidepressant drug, Prozac).

force and workplace of the 21st century. While, as a result of economic decline, this approach is being scaled back or abandoned in the companies (notably, Digital) that birthed it, some business leaders are asking, with Edward Simon, the President of Herman Miller, what is wrong with doing good works at work and improving the injustice that exists in the world. With the backing of such perceived power brokers, valuing differences may succeed. We need it not only in business but in education. In the classroom, it, in addition to *teaching away from* the ugly isms (racism, sexism . . .), certainly a primary function, means recognizing and appreciating *individual* differences and applying theories of cognitive development, optimum learning stages, and the functioning of the brain to help every individual and from birth. Those of us in this room probably will accept that American industry can reassert itself through the combination of Total Quality and this new emphasis on human rights and preparation for changes in the workforce and workplace that emphasize valuing differences. The latter makes the American approach unique. Those of us in this room probably will accept that we need diversity management and psychological safety in every workplace, including the academic. We need to share those views with the rest of the campus.

While we in higher education benefit from philanthropy (as so many of us have from George Eastman, for example, of Eastman Kodak) rather than practice it, we are simply not doing a very good job of the *spiritual* philanthropy that we can do—the leadership for change and particularly *moral* change. The college/university must have vision and must lead, not follow, society; its administrators must lead and not just manage. The greatest plight of higher education today is not the spiraling costs, as horrendous as they are, but the dearth of vision, one of the prime ingredients of the Total Quality Movement. The work of higher education ought to be to improve and uplift individuals and thence the society in which all of us live. At the present, it, rather, seems too often to mirror the violence, the giving over of the self to drugs and alcohol, the intolerance, and many other current harms that undermine us daily. We must center higher education again on its tasks: not only preparation for careers but preparation for full humanity. Adapting some thoughts of United States Senator Terry Sanford, the former President of Duke and a mentor of mine, I would say that higher education has forgotten its obligation to be a foe of human meanness and to enlist in the great causes of the nation and humankind. We can hone again the valuing of difference, creativity, problem-solving, ethics, and fair play. We must operate from a strong moral base. And, yes, we must find ways to value all differences; we must help those who have been dominant heretofore feel that they, too, are valued.

In this period of what I call the "new racism," the community colleges may be the ones who can do most about preparing minority students so that they are not driven into despair or violence by what they must confront but have a strong sense of self fostered by professional and caring individuals in the classrooms and the halls of their campuses. In 1988, you had 55% of the Hispanic, 57% of the Native American, 43% of the Black, and 42% of the Asian undergraduates in this country. The percentages are probably higher now.

From the broad moral sweep, someone needs to move more precisely to Total Quality, though its roots will have been exposed already in the foregoing. As one example, the campus needs to hear Dr. Deming's beliefs in the necessity not only for a new system of management but a different *spirit*; in the entitlement of all humans to have fun and to have joy in learning and in work; in the necessity for keeping all minds in a "learning mode." It needs to hear Dr. Deming say that what we have now is "win-lose" and that what we need is "win-win." It needs to be brought to his view of education: "I would rather have a pupil present to me a paper in which he gave reasons why a certain answer to a certain question could be right, and under what condition it could be wrong, and why another answer could be right or could be wrong. That would require him to think. It would give him a chance to think. He would develop some understanding of the world, why something is right or wrong. That would require him to think, and it would require the teacher to read the papers. What are we trying to create? Children that can think, or children that can carry in their heads a pile of information?"

Academics need to reflect on industry in such lights. Not only will they feel better about business; they may do something about *changing* themselves!

If an outsider or the President cannot perform these roles on your campus, you might try having all of the faculty and staff (and at least student representatives) read and discuss Peter Senge's *The Fifth Discipline*. I recommend that you do so even if you have access to the proper speakers. In an attempt to work on multiple levels (as well as because of the natural fit), Senge uses the language of education: "learning organization," organizations with "learning disabilities," "the child learner within us all," and "core disciplines," among others. His "localness" takes participatory and site-based management to new levels and into the extraordinary changes that must take place in leaders if real shared vision and shared leadership (no easier in education than in industry) are to prevail. This MIT business guru "legitimizes" education at the same time that he deplores its flaws (e.g., linear thinking, learning as the taking in of information, *survival* and *adaptive* rather than *generative* learning). He integrates and, in so doing, also legitimizes the "soft," including the mystical, with *metanoia* (shift of mind), transcendence, rapport between conscious and unconscious, and archetypes. Unfortunately, team learning, the woof and weave of TQM, is ultra foreign to academia.

Senge can help, as can you by pointing out such kindred efforts as team teaching and interdisciplinary studies. He is particularly good on team learning and on the microworlds of computer simulation that enhance long-term thinking by letting us see cause and effect that are ordinarily displaced by time. But the great breakthrough of *The Fifth Discipline* is the chapter on "The Leader's New Work" as designer, steward, and *teacher.*

We are hearing much of the reshaping of physics through the *dialogue* of great scientists. Senge describes the special kind of dialogue, explored by physicist David Bohm (who recently died), being practiced in the *learning* organization.[24] This "Sengean dialogue," as I term it, is a form of team learning, and its techniques or "science" must be practiced. It begins with—but moves beyond—people and ideas in conflict. Our campuses need to include workshops on Sengean dialogue. Conflict resolution is a 21st-century skill. It has to be a part of TQM.

If some business models can help us with the *qualitative,* others can help us with the *quantitative.* TQM efficiencies and economies enable us to discipline campus costs, in turn curbing the spiraling tuitions that are hurting students, their families, and all those who would seek a college degree. Important, too, is the fact that its doctrine of variation blurs the lines between quantitative and qualitative. If such matters do not make business palatable to education, nothing will.

---

[24]The Win/Win approach of Brazilian Paulo Freire is a kindred movement away from game-playing and to collaboration.

APPENDIX C:
Letter From New Jersey,
Dated April 4, 1993

Dear Ms. Sadler:

I heard of your work through *Aero-Gramme*, issue #9, from which I obtained the address this is mailed to.

I understand you are trying to combine Deming's Total Quality Management with holistic educational approaches.

I am attempting to combine current Quality Management principles with holistic ethical and self-improvement approaches. That is, I am a manager at AT&T, a serious student of my profession (management) and a serious student of natural philosophy.

You would greatly please me with any correspondence you might send me. A personal note would be a singular honor.

Few of us are striving to bring both sides of the brain (the yin and the yang of consciousness) to bear. Most favor one side or the other. Let us unite the parallel energies and reclaim our power, as whole and effective agents of change!   .   .   .

P.S.   If I can assist you in any way, even as just a sounding-board for your ideas, consider me signed-up and ready to start.

WORKS CITED

Bolter, Jay David. "*Locus*: A Computer Program for Topographic Writing." *Computer-Assisted Composition Journal* 6.2 (1992): 15–23.
———. *Writing Space: The Computer, Hypertext, and the History of Writing*. Hillsdale, NJ: Lawrence Erlbaum, 1991.
Bolter, Jay David, Michael Joyce, and John B. Smith. *Storyspace*. Cambridge, MA: Eastgate Systems.
Cool Hand Luke. Dir. Stuart Rosenberg. 1967.
Elbow, Peter. *Embracing Contraries: Explorations in Learning and Teaching*. New York: Oxford UP, 1986.
———. *Writing with Power: Techniques for Mastering the Writing Process*. New York: Oxford UP, 1986.
Field of Dreams. Dir. Phil Alden Robinson. 1989.
Gilstrap, Tracy A. "Collaborative Computer-Assisted Composition Classrooms: The Solution to the Classical Problems." *Computer-Assisted Composition Journal* 5.3 (1991): 52–53.
Hocking, Joan. "Suggestions for Using the Microcomputer to Teach Revision." *Computer-Assisted Composition Journal* 4.3 (1990): 68–73.
Hunter, Lynn Dean. "Teaching A Hippo To Dance: Creative Writers and the Composition Curriculum." Presentation at the AWP Pedagogy Forum. *Small College Creativity*. In press.
The Jayhawkers. Dir. Melvin Frank. 1959.

Kafka, Franz. *The Penal Colony.* Trans. Willa and Edwin Muir. New York: Schocken, 1984.

McAfee, Christine O'Leary. "Cognitive Readability and Desktop Publishing." *Computer-Assisted Composition Journal* 6.2 (1992): 33–36.

Maddox, Bruno. "Bookshelf: *E. M. Forster: A Biography* By Nicola Beauman." *Wall Street Journal* 2 June 1994: A12.

Miller, Michael W. "A Story of the Type That Turns Heads in Computer Circles: Digital Smiley Faces Are Used In E-Mail Conversations By the Lateral-Minded." *Wall Street Journal* 15 Sept. 1992: A1+.

Mollner, Terry. *The Relationship Age: The Emergence of a New Kind of Nation.* Shutesbury, MA: Trusteeship Institute, Inc., 1991.

Ong, Walter. *Orality and Literacy: The Technologizing of the Word.* New York: Methuen, 1982.

Panetta, Clayann Gilliam. "Computer-Assisted Composition: A Classical Interpretation." *Computer-Assisted Composition Journal* 5.3 (1991): 59–64.

Pope, Alexander. *An Essay on Criticism. A Collection of English Poems 1660–1800.* Ed. Ronald S. Crane. New York: Harper & Row, 1932.

Reynolds, John Frederick. "Classical Rhetoric and Computer-Assisted Composition: Extra-Textual Features as Delivery." *Computer-Assisted Composition Journal* 3.3 (1989): 101–07.

———. "Desktop Publishing and Technical Writing: Problems and Strategies." *Computer-Assisted Composition Journal* 5.1 (1990): 18–22.

Roberts, David H. "Writing: A Process That Can Be Improved." *Quality Quest in the Academic Process.* Ed. John W. Harris and J. Mark Baggett. Birmingham, AL: Samford U and GOAL/QPC, 1992. 159–69.

Russell, Bill, and Taylor Branch. *Second Wind: The Memoirs of an Opinionated Man.* New York: Random House, 1979.

Sadler, Lynn Veach. "Collaboration for Total Quality Education." Seminar on "Educational Leadership for a Competitive America," U.S. Office of Personnel Management, Central Management Development Center, Oak Ridge, TN, 8–19 June 1992.

———. "Genial Iconoclasm: A Call for Moving beyond Competition to Collaboration and Quality." "Quality and Education: Critical Linkages," A National Invitational Conference on Total Quality Management and the National Education Goals, Houston, TX, 9–10 November 1992.

———. "Some Recommendations for Education (and All of Us): Valuing Differences as Collaboration Beyond Outcomes Assessment and Total Quality Management/Demingism." Conference on "Creating the Quality School," U of Oklahoma, 30 March–1 April 1992. ERIC Clearinghouse on Educational Management, University of Oregon. ED 346 606.

———. "Then Came PC." 1994 North Carolina Writers' Network Poetry Competition.

———. "Total Quality Education and the Issues of Change." A National Invitational Conference on Total Quality Management and the National Education Goals, Denver, CO, 8–9 November 1993.

———. "Total Quality Management: The Issues of Change." "TQM and Education: A Conference for the Community College System of North Carolina," Southwestern Community College, Sylva, NC, 19–20 April 1993.

Sadler, Lynn Veach, and Wendy Tibbetts Greene. "Computer Applications for Writing: The Computer-Assisted Composition Movement." *ABACUS: The Magazine for the Computer Professional* 5.3 (1988): 22–33.

Sadler, Lynn Veach, Wendy Tibbetts Greene, and Emory W. Sadler. *Diagrammatic Writing Using Word Processing.* Fayetteville, NC: Methodist College, 1985.

Selfe, Cynthia L. "Computer-Based Conferences and the Non-Traditional English Classroom" [Abstract]. *Computer-Assisted Composition Journal* 3.1 (1988): 50.

Senge, Peter. *The Fifth Discipline: The Art & Practice of the Learning Organization.* New York: Doubleday/Currency, 1990.

The Works of John Milton. Ed. Frank Allen Patterson et al. New York: Columbia UP, 1931–38. 18 vols. in 21.

About the Authors

John Frederick Reynolds is Professor of English at The City College of The City University of New York (CUNY), where he teaches a variety of courses in rhetoric and composition studies. He received BA and MA degrees in speech communication and English from Midwestern (Texas) State University, and a PhD in composition studies from the University of Oklahoma, where he held the position of Visiting Lecturer from 1978 to 1988. His work has appeared in such professional journals as *College English, Rhetoric Review,* the *Rhetoric Society Quarterly,* the *Technical Communication Quarterly,* the *Computer-Assisted Composition Journal,* and the *Journal of Advanced Composition,* for which he served as Book Review Editor from 1989 to 1994. He is the editor of *Rhetoric, Cultural Studies, and Literacy: Selected Papers from the 1994 Conference of the Rhetoric Society of America* (Lawrence Erlbaum Associates, 1995) and *Rhetorical Memory and Delivery: Classical Concepts for Contemporary Composition and Communication* (Lawrence Erlbaum Associates, 1993); with David C. Mair and Pamela C. Fischer, he is the author of *Writing and Reading Mental Health Records: Issues and Analysis* (Sage Publications, 1992), which was nominated for an NCTE award for Best Book in Technical and Scientific Communication. From 1988 until 1994, Dr. Reynolds taught at Old Dominion University in Norfolk, Virginia, where he was twice a finalist for the Robert L. Stern Award for Excellence in Teaching, and served at various times in such capacities as Director of Writing Consultation Programs, Director of Advanced Composition Programs, Director of Computer Lab and Writing Associates Programs,

Director of Graduate Studies in Professional Writing, and Director of Under-graduate Studies in English. Dr. Reynolds previously held positions in corporate communications and preparatory-school teaching, debate coaching, and administration. He has been a consultant to NASA, the Boeing Company, and Norfolk Southern Corporation, among others.

Carolyn B. Matalene is Professor of English at the University of South Carolina (USC), where she has taught rhetoric, writing, and literature courses for the past 20 years, directed both undergraduate and graduate composition programs, and five times been a finalist for USC's Teacher of the Year Award, which she received in 1981. She earned a BA degree in English at Northwestern University, and MA and PhD degrees in English at the University of Pennsylvania. Prior to joining the faculty at USC, she taught at Benedict College, South Carolina State College, and The City College of CUNY. She has published more than two dozen scholarly articles, presented more than three dozen papers at academic conferences and conventions, developed the computer software *LiveWriter* in collaboration with Robert L. Oakman and Robert L. Cannon, served as editor of the quarterly *Carolina Writer*, and edited the collection *Worlds of Writing: Teaching and Learning in Discourse Communities of Work* (Random House, 1989), one of the first books in rhetoric and composition studies to explore the nature of discourse in non-academic settings. Dr. Matalene has received numerous grants, honors, and awards, including an Exchange Professorship at Shanxi University in the People's Republic of China; a Visiting Professorship at the American Cooperative School in Monrovia, Liberia; and a Fulbright Exchange Professorship, as well as a Donner Research Professorship, at Abo Akademi in Turku, Finland. She has been a writing coach for Columbia Newspapers since 1985, a gubernatorial appointee to several South Carolina state advisory commissions and task forces, and has three times been appointed to the faculty of the Poynter Institute for Media Studies in St. Petersburg, Florida.

Joyce Neff Magnotto is Assistant Professor of English at Old Dominion University in Norfolk, Virginia, where she teaches various writing courses, mentors graduate students in both composition pedagogy and professional writing, and directs the English department's Teletechnet program for televised writing instruction. Previously she taught English and humanities, co-ordinated writing across the curriculum efforts, and chaired the writing department at Prince George's Community College in Largo, Maryland. She received her BA in English from Western Maryland College, her MA in English from the University of Maryland at College Park, and her PhD in writing from the University of Pennsylvania, where her doctoral dissertation was a finalist for CCCC's Outstanding Dissertation Award. Dr. Magnotto has extensive experience developing and teaching writing courses for state and federal agencies. She has taught for the U.S. Department of Labor, the U.S. Office of Government Ethics, the Georgia State Auditors, and the U.S. General

Accounting Office, for whom she has been a consultant since 1987. She has taught on-site workshops at regional offices all across the country, as well as special seminars to multiple sites simultaneously via interactive television. Her work has appeared in such journals as *The MAHE Journal*, the *Composition Chronicle*, the *Journal of Advanced Composition*, and *College Composition and Communication*, and in various books, including *Writing Across the Curriculum: A Guide to Developing Programs* (Sage Publications, 1992), *Programs That Work: Models and Methods for Writing Across the Curriculum* (Boynton/Cook, 1990), and *Strengthening Programs in Writing Across the Curriculum* (Jossey-Bass, 1988). In 1993, Dr. Magnotto was elected to the National Nominating Committee of the CCCC, and received a Fulbright-Hays Fellowship for summer study in China.

Donald C. Samson, Jr. is Associate Professor of English at Radford University in Radford, Virginia, where he teaches courses in technical writing, technical editing, and American literature, and coaches the men's rugby team. Earlier he taught technical writing and Shakespeare at Eastern Michigan University, and technical writing, British literature, and film studies at the University of Tennessee. He holds a BA in English from Cornell University, and an MA and PhD in English from the University of North Carolina at Chapel Hill. Dr. Samson began his work in technical writing in 1965 as a writer for the Crouse-Hinds Company of Syracuse, New York, for whom he wrote foundry, machining, and assembly/operation instructions for the manufacture of outdoor lighting and traffic-signal equipment. After completing his doctorate and teaching for several years, he worked for 2 years as a Senior Writer/Editor for Martin Marietta Electronics and Missile Systems in Orlando, Florida, where he designed and edited proposals, reports, and briefing materials, primarily on Department of Defense projects. He edited volumes of successful major proposals—for the Management of the Department of Energy facilities in Oak Ridge, Tennessee; the Supersonic Low Altitude Target program; the multinational Multiple Launch Rocket System Terminal Guidance Warhead program; the Outer Air Battle Weapon System program; and the HELLFIRE Modular Missile System program. He also edited classified reports on such subjects as laser vibration sensing, fiberoptic gyros, artificial intelligence, target acquisition, and missile survivability. In 1993, Oxford University Press published Dr. Samson's book *Editing Technical Writing*. His articles have appeared in *Technical Communication, The Technical Writing Teacher, IEEE Transactions on Professional Communication*, and the *Journal of Technical Writing and Communication*. He has spoken on writing at the CCCC, the NCTE, the Society for Technical Communication, and other academic conferences.

Lynn Veach Sadler is founder and editor-in-chief of Human Technology Interface Ink Press, which publishes, among other things, *The Computer-Assisted Composition Journal, Small College Creativity*, and *MicroPsych Net-*

work. Previously she was President of Johnson State College in Johnson, Vermont. Earlier she was Professor of English, Dean of the College, and Vice-President for Academic Affairs at Methodist College in Fayetteville, North Carolina; before that, Chair of the Department of Communications and Dean of the Division of Humanities at Bennett College; and earlier, an English professor at Drake University, A & T State University, and Agnes Scott College. She earned a BA in English from Duke University, and an MA and PhD in English from the University of Illinois. Originally a Miltonist, Dr. Sadler has—in addition to several novels, short stories, and poems—written five scholarly books, edited 10 academic books or conference proceedings, and published about six dozen research articles on literature, composition, computers, and higher education. She currently speaks and consults extensively on such topics as issues facing education in the 21st century, diversity and pluralism, valuing differences, shared governance, computer applications in education, Total Quality Management, and Total Quality Education. Among her many accomplishments, Dr. Sadler received an Extraordinary Undergraduate Teaching Award at Drake University, was a pioneer in computer-assisted composition, and in 1991 gave the keynote address at the College English Association. She is currently revising her novel *Tonight I Lie with William Cullen Bryant,* which was selected for the 1993 Blumenthal Writers and Readers Series, and enjoying the attention she has received of late for her "The Land of Porkahontas," a comic poem promoting whole-hog barbecue as the state food of North Carolina.

Author Index